Twenty-Four
Hours a Day

for Teens

HAZELDEN®

Hazelden
Center City, Minnesota 55012-0176

1-800-328-0094
1-651-213-4590 (Fax)
www.hazelden.org

Library of Congress Cataloging-in-Publication Data

    Twenty-four hours a day for teens.
      p. cm.
    ISBN 13: 978-1-59285-078-5   ISBN 10: 1-59285-078-2
    1. Teenagers—Prayer-books and devotions—English.
  2. Alcoholics—Prayer-books and devotions—English.
  3. Devotional calendars.   I. Hazelden Foundation.
    BV4531.3.T94 2004
    204'.32—dc22

                                    2003062499

07 06   6 5 4 3 2

Editor's note
Twenty-Four Hours a Day for Teens is an abridged and
revised version of *Twenty-Four Hours a Day*. The original
version of *Twenty-Four Hours a Day* was compiled by a
member of the Group at Daytona Beach, Florida.

Cover design by David Spohn
Interior design by David Spohn
Typesetting by Stanton Publication Servies, Inc.

Foreword

Twenty-Four Hours a Day for Teens is intended to help members of Alcoholics Anonymous in their program of living one day at a time. It is designed for those who want to start each day with a few minutes of thought, meditation, and prayer.

These daily readings contain most of the material used in the booklet "For Drunks Only" and other AA literature, as well as some passages from the Big Book, *Alcoholics Anonymous*.

As a basis for the meditations in this book, the author has used many passages from the book *God Calling* by Two Listeners, edited by A. J. Russell. Permission to use the universal spiritual thoughts expressed in this book, without using direct quotations, has been granted by Dodd, Mead & Co., New York City.

The author hopes that these daily readings may help members of Alcoholics Anonymous find the power they need to stay sober each twenty-four hours. If we don't take that first drink today, we'll never take it, because it's always today.

Look to this day,
For it is life,
The very life of life.
In its brief course lie all
The realities and verities of existence,
The bliss of growth,
The splendor of action,
The glory of power—

For yesterday is but a dream,
And tomorrow is only a vision,
But today, well lived,
Makes every yesterday a dream of happiness
And every tomorrow a vision of hope.

Look well, therefore, to this day.

Sanskrit proverb
by Kalidasa,
Indian poet and playwright,
Fourth century A.D.

Hazelden Publishing and Educational Services is a division of the Hazelden Foundation, a not-for-profit organization. Since 1949, Hazelden has been a leader in promoting the dignity and treatment of people afflicted with the disease of chemical dependency.

The mission of the foundation is to improve the quality of life for individuals, families, and communities by providing a national continuum of information, education, and recovery services that are widely accessible; to advance the field through research and training; and to improve our quality and effectiveness through continuous improvement and innovation.

Stemming from that, the mission of this division is to provide quality information and support to people wherever they may be in their personal journey— from education and early intervention, through treatment and recovery, to personal and spiritual growth.

Although our treatment programs do not necessarily use everything Hazelden publishes, our bibliotherapeutic materials support our mission and the Twelve Step philosophy upon which it is based. We encourage your comments and feedback.

The headquarters of the Hazelden Foundation are in Center City, Minnesota. Additional treatment facilities are located in Chicago, Illinois; Newberg, Oregon; New York, New York; Plymouth, Minnesota; and St. Paul, Minnesota. At these sites, we provide a continuum of care for men and women of all ages. Our Plymouth facility is designed specifically for youth and families.

For more information on Hazelden,
please call **1-800-257-7800.**

Or you may access our World Wide Web site
on the Internet at **www.hazelden.org.**

Twenty-Four Hours a Day

for Teens

JANUARY

AA Thought for the Day

 When we came into Alcoholics Anonymous, were we desperate? Were we so sick of ourselves and our way of living that we couldn't stand looking at ourselves in a mirror? Were we ready to try anything that would help us to get sober and to get over our soul-sickness? *Should I ever forget the condition I was in?*

Meditation for the Day

In the new year, I will live one day at a time. I will make each day one of preparation for better things ahead. I will not dwell on the past or the future, only on the present. I will bury every fear of the future.

Prayer for the Day

I pray that God will guide me one day at a time in the new year. I pray that for each day, God will supply the wisdom and the strength that I need.

AA Thought for the Day

What makes AA work? We must admit that alcohol had us licked and that we want to quit the old life. Then we must surrender our life to a Higher Power, put our drinking problem in his hands and leave it there. After these things are done, we should attend meetings regularly. We should also try to help other alcoholics. *Am I doing these things?*

Meditation for the Day

God has promised to help with the burdens of the day only. If I am foolish enough to gather again that burden of the past and carry it, then indeed I cannot expect God to help me bear it. So I forget that which lies behind me and breathe in the blessing of each new day.

Prayer for the Day

I pray that I may realize that, for good or bad, past days have ended.

AA Thought for the Day

When we came into AA, we learned what an alcoholic was and then we applied this knowledge to ourselves to see we were alcoholics. Have we admitted openly that we are alcoholics? *Am I ready to admit it at any time when I can be of help?*

Meditation for the Day

I will be renewed. I will be remade. In this, I need God's help. His spirit will flow through me, and, in flowing through me, it will sweep away all the bitter past. Each day will unfold something good, as long as I am trying to live the way I believe God wants me to live.

Prayer for the Day

I pray that I may be taught, just as a child would be taught. I pray that I may never question God's plans, but accept them gladly.

AA Thought for the Day

Have we accepted the fact that we must spend the rest of our lives without liquor? Do we have any more reservations, any idea in the back of our mind that someday we'll be able to drink safely? *Am I absolutely honest with myself and with other people?*

Meditation for the Day

I believe that fundamentally all is well. Good things will happen to me. I believe that God cares for me and will provide for me.

Prayer for the Day

I pray that I will not try to carry the burden of the universe on my shoulders. I pray that I may be satisfied to do my share each day.

AA Thought for the Day

Have we turned to a Higher Power for help? Do we believe that this Higher Power can keep us from drinking? Do we ask God to give us the power to stay sober for each twenty-four hours? *Do I attend AA meetings regularly?*

Meditation for the Day

I believe that God's presence brings peace and that peace, like a quiet-flowing river, will cleanse all irritants away. In these quiet times, I will not be afraid. When I am relaxed, God's strength will flow into me. I will be at peace.

Prayer for the Day

I pray for that peace which passes all understanding. I pray for that peace which the world can neither give nor take away.

AA Thought for the Day

 Keeping sober is the most important thing in our lives. We are convinced that our lives depend on not taking that first drink. Nothing in the world is as important to us as our own sobriety. Everything we have, our whole lives, depends on that one thing. *Can I afford ever to forget this, even for one minute?*

Meditation for the Day

I will discipline myself. I know that the goodness of my life is a necessary foundation for its usefulness.

Prayer for the Day

I pray that I may face and accept whatever discipline is necessary. I pray that I may be fit to receive God's power in my life.

AA Thought for the Day

 When temptation comes, as it does sometimes to all of us, we will say to ourselves, *No, our whole lives depend on not taking that drink and nothing in the world can make us do it.* We've given up our right to drink and it's not our decision any longer. *Have I made the choice once and for all, so that there's no going back on it?*

Meditation for the Day

God's word is spoken to the secret places of my heart and, in some hour of temptation, I find that word and realize its value for the first time.

Prayer for the Day

I pray that I may see God's meaning in my life.

AA Thought for the Day

Saint Paul once said that nothing in the world, neither powers nor principalities, neither life nor death, could separate him from the love of God. *Once I have given my drinking problem to God, should anything in the world separate me from my sobriety?*

Meditation for the Day

I know that my new life will not be immune from difficulties, but I will have peace even in difficulties. I know that serenity is the result of faithful, trusting acceptance of God's will, even in the midst of difficulties.

Prayer for the Day

I pray that I may welcome difficulties. I pray that they may test my strength and build my character.

AA Thought for the Day

 When we were drinking, most of us had no real faith in anything. But when we came into AA, we began to have faith in God. And we found that faith gave us the strength we needed to overcome drinking. *Have I learned that there is strength in faith?*

Meditation for the Day

I will have faith, no matter what may befall me. I will be patient, even in the midst of troubles. I will not fear the strain of life, because I believe that God knows just what I can bear. I know that God will not ask me to bear anything that could overcome or destroy me.

Prayer for the Day

I pray that I may put this day in the hands of God.

AA Thought for the Day

When we were drinking, most of us were full of pride and selfishness. We believed we could handle our own affairs, even though we were making a mess of our lives. We were very stubborn and didn't like to take advice. We resented being told what to do. To us, humility looked like weakness. But when we came into AA, we began to be humble. *Have I learned that there is power in humility?*

Meditation for the Day

I will come to God in faith, and he will give me a new way of life. This new way of life will alter my whole existence, the words I speak, the influence I have.

Prayer for the Day

I pray that I may learn the principles of the good life. I pray that I may meditate upon them and work at them, because they are eternal.

AA Thought for the Day

 When we were drinking, most of us never thought of helping others. We liked to offer drinks to our friends because that made us feel like big shots. But we only used others for our own pleasure. To really go out and try to help somebody who needed help never occurred to us. But when we came into AA, we found out that helping others made us happy and also helped us to stay sober. *Have I learned that there is happiness in helping others?*

Meditation for the Day

I will pray only for strength and that God's will be done.

Prayer for the Day

I pray that I may seek God's guidance day by day.

AA Thought for the Day

The longer we're in AA, the more natural this way of life seems. Our old drinking lives were a very unnatural way of living. During the early years of our drinking, our lives weren't so different from the lives of a lot of other people. But as we gradually became problem drinkers, our lives became more and more unnatural. *Do I realize now that the things I did were far from natural?*

Meditation for the Day

I will say thank you to God for everything, even the seeming trials and worries. I will strive to be grateful and humble. My whole attitude toward my Higher Power will be one of gratitude.

Prayer for the Day

I pray that I may be grateful for the things I have received and do not deserve. I pray that this gratitude will make me truly humble.

AA Thought for the Day

When we were drinking, we were living an unnatural life physically and mentally. We were punishing our bodies by loading them with alcohol. We didn't eat enough and we ate the wrong things. We didn't get enough sleep or the right kind of rest. We had an alcoholic obsession, and we couldn't imagine life without alcohol. We kept imagining all kinds of crazy things about ourselves and about other people. *Since I came into AA, am I getting better physically and mentally?*

Meditation for the Day

I will never despair or be despondent. I now have friends who long for me to conquer. If I should slip or fail, it would cause pain and disappointment to them. I will keep trying to live a better life.

Prayer for the Day

I pray that I may always call on God's strength.

AA Thought for the Day

When we first came into AA, a sober life seemed strange. We wondered what life could possibly be like without ever taking a drink. But the longer we're in AA, the more natural this way of life seems. And now we know that the life we're living in AA—the sobriety, the fellowship, the faith in God, and the trying to help each other—is the most natural way we could possibly live. *Do I believe it's the way God wants me to live?*

Meditation for the Day

I will learn to overcome myself, because every blow to selfishness is used to shape the real, eternal, unperishable me. It is not the difficulties of life that I have to conquer, so much as my own selfishness.

Prayer for the Day

I pray that I may obey God and walk with him and listen to him. I pray that I may strive to overcome my own selfishness.

AA Thought for the Day

 The Twelve Steps are like guideposts. They point the direction in which we have to go. But all members of the group have to find their own best way to live the program. We don't all do it exactly alike. *Has the AA way become my regular, natural way of living?*

Meditation for the Day

I will relax and not get tense. I will have no fear, because everything will work out in the end. I will claim God's power and use it, because if I do not use it, it will be withdrawn.

Prayer for the Day

I pray that I may relax and that God's strength will be given to me. I pray that I may subject my will to God's will and be free from all tenseness.

AA Thought for the Day

The AA program is more a way of building a new life than just a way of getting over drinking, because in AA we don't just stop drinking. We did that plenty of times in the old days when we "went on the wagon." And, of course, we always started to drink again, because we were only waiting for the time when we could fall off. *Am I going uphill, getting better and better?*

Meditation for the Day

I believe that God is Lord of little things, the Divine Controller of little happenings. I will persevere in this new way of life. I know that nothing in the day is too small to be part of God's scheme.

Prayer for the Day

I pray that the little stones that I put into the mosaic of my life may make a worthwhile pattern.

AA Thought for the Day

 It doesn't do much good to come to meetings only once in awhile and sit around, hoping to get something out of the program. That's all right at first, but it won't help us very long. Sooner or later we have to get into action by coming to meetings regularly, by giving a personal witness of our experience with alcohol, and by trying to help other alcoholics. *Am I spending time and effort on the new life that I'm trying to build in AA?*

Meditation for the Day

When one worrying or impatient thought enters my mind, I will put it out at once. I know that love and trust are the solvents for the worry and troubles of life. I will use them to form a protective screen around me.

Prayer for the Day

I pray that troubles and impatience and worry will not wear away my protective screen. I pray that I may banish all of these from my life.

AA Thought for the Day

The new life can't be built in a day. We have to take the program slowly, a little at a time. Our subconscious minds have to be reeducated. We have to learn to think differently. We have to get used to sober thinking instead of alcoholic thinking. *Am I building a new life on the foundation of sobriety?*

Meditation for the Day

I will pray daily for faith, for it is God's gift. It is a necessary weapon for overcoming all adverse conditions and for accomplishment of all good in my life.

Prayer for the Day

I pray that I may so think and live as to feed my faith in God. I pray that my faith may grow, because with faith God's power becomes available to me.

AA Thought for the Day

On the foundation of sobriety, we can build a life of honesty, unselfishness, faith in God, and love of our fellow human beings. We'll never fully reach these goals, but the adventure of building that kind of a life is so much better than the merry-go-round of our old drinking life that there's no comparison. *Am I living the way of honesty, unselfishness, and faith?*

Meditation for the Day

I believe that God had already seen my heart's needs before I cried to him, before I was conscious of those needs myself. I believe that God was already preparing the answer.

Prayer for the Day

I pray that I may understand my real wants and needs. I pray that my understanding of those needs and wants may help to bring the answer to them.

AA Thought for the Day

In AA we're all through with lying, hangovers, remorse, and wasting money. When we were drinking, we were only half alive. Now that we're trying to live decent, honest, unselfish lives, we're really alive. *Am I convinced that no matter how much fun I got out of drinking, that life never was as good as the life I can build in AA?*

Meditation for the Day

I want to be at one with the Divine Spirit of the universe. I will set my deepest affections on things spiritual, not on things material. No human aspiration can reach higher than this.

Prayer for the Day

I pray that I may think love, and love will surround me. I pray that I may think health, and health will come to me.

AA Thought for the Day

To grasp the AA program, we have to change from alcoholic thinking to sober thinking. Before we came into AA, we wanted an artificial life of excitement and everything that goes with drinking. That kind of a life looked normal to us then. But as we look back now, that life looks most abnormal. We must reeducate our minds. *Am I changing from an abnormal thinker to a normal thinker?*

Meditation for the Day

I will take the most crowded day without fear. I believe that God is with me and controlling all. I will not get worried, because I know that God is my helper. Underneath are the everlasting arms. I will rest in them.

Prayer for the Day

I pray that I may be calm and let nothing upset me.

AA Thought for the Day

After awhile, we get so that we really enjoy simple, healthy, normal living. We really get a kick out of life without the artificial stimulus of alcohol. All we have to do is to look around at the members of any AA group and we will see how their outlook has changed. *Is my outlook on life changing?*

Meditation for the Day

I will never forget to say thank you to God, even on the grayest days. My attitude will be one of humility and gratitude. Saying thank you to God is a daily practice that is absolutely necessary. If a day is not one of thankfulness, the practice has to be repeated until it becomes so. Gratitude is a necessity for those who seek to live a better life.

Prayer for the Day

I pray that gratitude will bring humility. I pray that humility will bring me to live a better life.

AA Thought for the Day

Active alcoholics are people whose drinking got them into a blind alley. They haven't been able to learn anything from their drinking experiences. They are always making the same mistakes and suffering the same consequences. They still think they can handle the stuff. They won't face the fact that they must spend the rest of their lives without liquor. They can't visualize life without ever taking a drink. *Am I out of this blind alley?*

Meditation for the Day

I believe that God has all power. It is breathed in by the person who lives in God's presence. I will learn to live in God's presence, and then I will have those things that I desire of him: strength, power, and joy.

Prayer for the Day

I pray that I may get myself out of the way, so that God's power may flow in. I pray that I may surrender myself to that power.

AA Thought for the Day

Alcoholics who are living in a blind alley refuse to be really honest with themselves or with other people. They're running away from life and won't face things as they are. There's only one way to get out of that blind alleyway of living and that's to change our thinking. *Have I changed my thinking?*

Meditation for the Day

I know that I cannot see the road ahead. I must go just one step at a time, because God does not grant me a longer view.

Prayer for the Day

I pray that I may learn that trying to do God's will is perfect freedom.

AA Thought for the Day

 We depended on drinking to help us enjoy things. It broke down our shyness and helped us to have a "good time." We depended on drinking to help us when we felt low physically. If we had a hangover, we felt better after a few drinks. We depended on drinking to help us when we felt low mentally. If we'd had a tough day at school, we felt better under the influence of alcohol. For us alcoholics, it got so that we depended on drinking for almost everything. *Have I gotten over that dependence on drinking?*

Meditation for the Day

I believe that complete surrender of my life to God is the foundation of serenity. I believe that the kingdom of God is within us and we can enjoy "eternal life" here and now.

Prayer for the Day

I pray that understanding, insight, and vision to make my life eternal, here and now, will be mine.

AA Thought for the Day

As we became alcoholics, the bad effects of drinking came more and more to outweigh the good effects. But no matter what drinking did to us, we depended on it. Our dependence on drinking became an obsession. Now we learn how to change from alcoholic thinking to sober thinking. And we find that we can no longer depend on drinking for anything. We depend on a Higher Power instead. *Have I entirely given up that dependence on drinking?*

Meditation for the Day

No matter what fears, worries, and resentments I may have, I must try to think of constructive things, until calmness comes. Only when I am calm can I act as a channel for God's spirit.

Prayer for the Day

I pray that I may build up instead of tear down.
I pray that I may be constructive and
not destructive.

AA Thought for the Day

What a load lying puts on our shoulders! Drinking makes liars out of all of us alcoholics. We have to lie about where we've been and what we've been doing. When we are lying we are only half alive, because of the fear of being found out. When we get honest with ourselves and with other people, that terrible load of lying falls off our shoulders. *Have I gotten rid of that load of lying?*

Meditation for the Day

I believe that in the spiritual world, as in the material world, there is no empty space. As fears and worries and resentments depart out of my life, the things of the spirit come in to take their places. As soon as I am rid of fears and hates and selfishness, God's love and peace and calm can come in.

Prayer for the Day

*I pray that I may rid myself of all fears
and resentments, so that peace and serenity may
take their place.*

AA Thought for the Day

What a load remorse puts on our shoulders! Ashamed of the things we've said and done. Afraid to face people because of what they might think of us. Afraid of the consequences of what we did when we were drunk. What an awful beating the mind takes! When we come into AA, that terrible load of remorse falls off our shoulders. *Have I gotten rid of remorse?*

Meditation for the Day

When I seek to follow the way of the spirit, I experience a complete reversal of the way of the world that I had previously followed. But it is a reversal that leads to happiness and peace.

Prayer for the Day

I pray that I will not be weary, disillusioned, or disappointed. I pray that I will not put my trust in the ways of the world, but in the way of the spirit.

AA Thought for the Day

It is said that members of AA have paid the highest initiation fee of any club members in the world, because we've wasted so much money on liquor. We'll never be able to figure out how much it was. We not only wasted our own money, but also the money of our families. But when we come into AA, we get a wonderful feeling of release and freedom. *Can I throw back my shoulders and look the whole world in the face again?*

Meditation for the Day

I believe that the future is in the hands of God. I am being led in a very definite way, as I try to rebuild my life. I am the builder, but God is the architect. It is mine to build as best I can, under his guidance.

Prayer for the Day

I pray that I may live my life as I believe God wants me to live it.

AA Thought for the Day

 A drinking life isn't a happy life. Drinking cuts us off from other people and from God. One of the worst things about drinking is the loneliness. And one of the best things about AA is the fellowship. Drinking cuts us off from other people, at least from the people who really matter to us. *Have I gotten rid of my loneliness?*

Meditation for the Day

I will sometimes go aside into a quiet place of retreat with God. In that place, I will find restoration and healing and power.

Prayer for the Day

I pray that I may strengthen my inner life, so that I may find serenity. I pray that my soul may be restored in quietness and peace.

AA Thought for the Day

 Drinking cuts us off from God. No matter how we were brought up, no matter what our religion is, no matter if we say we believe in God, nevertheless we build up a wall between us and God by our drinking. We know we're not living the way God wants us to. *Do I have real fellowship with other people and with God?*

Meditation for the Day

Can I trust God, no matter how low I feel? Can I say, "Thy will be done," no matter how much I am defeated? If I can, my faith is real and practical. It works in bad times as well as in good times. The Divine Will is working in a way that is beyond my finite mind to understand, but I can still trust in it.

Prayer for the Day

I pray that I may accept pain and defeat as part of God's plan for my spiritual growth.

FEBRUARY

AA Thought for the Day

 When we think about having a drink, we're thinking of the kick we get out of drinking, the pleasure, the escape from boredom, the feeling of self-importance, and the companionship of other drinkers. What we don't think of is the let-down, the hangover, the remorse, the waste of money, and the facing of another day. *Do I believe that the liabilities of drinking outweigh the assets?*

Meditation for the Day

I will start a new life each day. God always offers me a fresh start. If God's forgiveness were only for the righteous and those who had not sinned, where would be its need?

Prayer for the Day

I pray that my life may not be spoiled by worry and fear and selfishness. I pray that I may have a glad, thankful, and humble heart.

AA Thought for the Day

 We got a kick out of the first few drinks, before we got stupefied by alcohol. For a while, the world seemed to look brighter. But how about the letdown, the terrible depression that comes the morning after? In AA, we get a real kick: not a false feeling of exhilaration, but a real feeling of satisfaction with ourselves, self-respect, and a feeling of friendliness toward the world. *In AA, am I getting real pleasure and serenity and peace?*

Meditation for the Day

I will practice love, because lack of love will block the way. I will try to see good in all people. They are all children of God. I will try to get along with all people, because the more love I give away, the more I will have.

Prayer for the Day

I pray that I may do all I can to love others, in spite of their many faults.

FEBRUARY 3

AA Thought for the Day

 By drinking, we escaped from boredom for a while. We almost forgot our troubles. But when we sobered up, our troubles were twice as bad. Nobody's bored at an AA meeting. We stick around after it's over, and we hate to leave. Drinking gave us a temporary feeling of importance. In AA we don't want that kind of self-importance. We have real self-respect and honesty and humility. *Have I found something much better and more satisfactory than drinking?*

Meditation for the Day

I believe that my faith and God's power can accomplish anything in human relationships. There is no limit to what these two things can do in this field. If I only believe, anything can happen.

Prayer for the Day

I pray that I may try to strengthen my faith day by day. I pray that I may rely more and more on God's power.

AA Thought for the Day

Treating others to drinks gave us a kind of satisfaction. We liked to say, "Have a drink on me." But we were not really doing the other people a favor. We were only helping them to get drunk. In AA we really try to help other alcoholics. We make real friends, not fair-weather friends. *With sobriety, have I got everything that drinking's got, without the headaches?*

Meditation for the Day

I know that God cannot teach anyone who is trusting in a crutch. I will throw away the crutch of alcohol and walk in God's power and spirit. God's will shall be revealed to me as I go forward.

Prayer for the Day

I pray that I may throw away my alcoholic crutch and let God's power take its place.

AA Thought for the Day

 One thing we learn in AA is to take a long view of drinking instead of a short view. When we were drinking we thought more about the pleasure or release that a drink would give us than we did about the consequences that would result from our taking that drink. *Have I learned that what's inside those beautiful bottles is just plain poison to me?*

Meditation for the Day

I believe that life is a school in which I must learn spiritual things. I must trust in God and he will teach me. I must listen to God and he will speak through my mind. I must commune with him in spite of all opposition and every obstacle. If I persist, God will reveal himself to me in many ways.

Prayer for the Day

I pray that I may grow spiritually by making a practice of these things.

AA Thought for the Day

 On a dark night, the bright lights of a party look mighty inviting. Inside, there seems to be warmth and good cheer. But we don't stop to think that if we go in there we'll probably end up drunk, with an awful hangover. *Can I look straight through the night before and see the morning after?*

Meditation for the Day

God finds, amid the crowd, a few people who follow him, just to be near him, just to dwell in his presence. I will let God know that I seek just to dwell in his presence, to be near him, not so much for teaching or a message, as just for him. It may be that the longing of the human heart to be loved for itself is something caught from the Great Divine Heart.

Prayer for the Day

I pray that I may have a listening ear, so that God may speak to me. I pray that I may have a waiting heart, so that God may come to me.

AA Thought for the Day

A party crowded with people who are drinking looks like a very festive place. But if we were to see the place the next morning we'd see a mess! The fun of the night before is all gone and only the stink of the morning after is left. *Has the night before become less important to me and the morning after more important?*

Meditation for the Day

I am now walking in darkness, surrounded by the limitations of space and time. But even in this darkness, I can have faith. Only a cry from the heart, a trusting cry, pierces that darkness and reaches to the divine ear of God.

Prayer for the Day

I pray that the divine power of God will help my human weakness.

AA Thought for the Day

 When the morning sun comes up and we jump out of bed, we're thankful to God that we feel well and happy instead of sick and disgusted. Serenity and happiness have become much more important to us than the excitement of drinking. All of us alcoholics had a lot of fun with drinking. We might as well admit it. But the time comes when drinking ceases to be fun. *Have I learned that drinking can never again be anything but trouble for me?*

Meditation for the Day

I will wait for guidance on each important decision. I will meet the test of waiting until a thing seems right before I do it. Every work for God must meet this test of time. The guidance will come, if I wait for it.

Prayer for the Day

I pray that I may meet the test of waiting for God's guidance. I pray that I will not go off on my own.

AA Thought for the Day

When we came into AA, we found a lot of people who, like ourselves, had had fun with drinking, but who now admitted that liquor had become nothing but trouble for them. And when we found that this thing had happened to a lot of other people besides ourselves, we realized that perhaps we weren't such odd ducks after all. *Have I learned to admit that for me drinking has ceased to be fun and has become nothing but trouble?*

Meditation for the Day

The lifeline, the line of rescue, is the line from the soul to God. On one end of the lifeline is my faith and on the other end is God's power. I will trust in this lifeline and never be afraid. I will look to God and trust him when I am emotionally upset.

Prayer for the Day

I pray that I may keep a strong hold
on the lifeline of faith.

AA Thought for the Day

 In AA we learn the most important thing anyone can ever learn: that we can call on a Higher Power to help us keep away from liquor, that we can work with that Divine Principle in the universe, and that God will help us to live a sober, useful, happy life. So now we no longer care about the fact that we can never have any more fun with drinking. *Have I learned that I am much happier without it?*

Meditation for the Day

Like a tree, I must be pruned of a lot of dead branches before I will be ready to bear good fruit. There are new leaves, buds, blossoms, and fruit, many times better because of the pruning. I am in the hands of a Master Gardener, who makes no mistakes in his pruning.

Prayer for the Day

I pray that I may cut away the dead branches of my life. I pray that I will not mind the pruning, since it helps me to bear good fruit later.

AA Thought for the Day

If we're going to stay sober, we've got to learn to want something else more than we want to drink. When we first came into AA, we couldn't imagine wanting anything else so much as or more than drinking. So we had to stop drinking on faith, on faith that someday we really would want something else more than drinking. *Have I found that when I keep sober, everything goes well for me?*

Meditation for the Day

There is almost no work in life so difficult as waiting. And yet God wants me to wait. All motion is more easy than calm waiting, and yet I must wait until God shows me his will. If I wait patiently, preparing myself always, someday I will be at the place where I want to be.

Prayer for the Day

I pray that I may wait patiently. I pray that I may trust God and keep preparing myself for a better life.

AA Thought for the Day

 As we look back on all those troubles we used to have when we were drinking—the hospitals, the police— we wonder how we could have wanted that kind of a life. As we look back on it now, we see our drinking life as it really was, and we're glad we're out of it. So after a few months in AA, we find that we can honestly say that we want something else more than drinking. *Do I want to keep sober a lot more than I want to get drunk?*

Meditation for the Day

My spiritual life depends on an inner consciousness of God. If in every single happening, event, and plan I am conscious of God, then no matter what happens, I will be safe in God's hands.

Prayer for the Day

I pray that I may always have this consciousness of God.

AA Thought for the Day

Sometimes we can't help thinking, *Why can't we ever drink again?* The answer is that at some time in our drinking careers, we passed what is called our "tolerance point." We passed from a condition in which we could tolerate alcohol to a condition in which we could not tolerate it at all. After that, if we took one drink, we would sooner or later end up drunk. *When I think of liquor now, do I think of it as something that I can never tolerate again?*

Meditation for the Day

The goal of the spiritual life is in sight. All I need is the final effort. The saddest records are made by people who ran well, with brave, stout hearts, until the sight of the goal, and then some weakness or self-indulgence held them back. They never knew how near they were to victory.

Prayer for the Day

I pray that I may press on until the goal is reached. I pray that I will not give up in the final stretch.

AA Thought for the Day

After that first drink, we had a single-track mind. It was like a railroad train. The first drink started it off, and it kept going on the single track until it got to the end of the line, drunkenness. It's not the second drink or the tenth drink that does the damage. It's the first drink. *Will I ever take that first drink again?*

Meditation for the Day

I must keep a time apart with God every day. Gradually I will be transformed mentally and spiritually. It is not the praying so much as just being in God's presence. The strengthening and healing powers of this I cannot understand, but my greatest spiritual growth occurs in this time apart with God.

Prayer for the Day

I pray that I may faithfully keep a quiet time apart with God. I pray that I may grow spiritually each day.

AA Thought for the Day

 Alcoholism is not just a physical allergy. It's also a mental allergy or obsession. After we've become alcoholics, we can still tolerate alcohol physically for quite a while, although we suffer a little more after each binge, and each time it takes a little longer to get over the hangovers. *Do I realize that since I have become an alcoholic, I cannot tolerate alcohol mentally at all?*

Meditation for the Day

I let inspiration take the place of aspiration. I seek to grow spiritually, rather than to acquire fame and riches. My chief ambition is to be used by God. The Divine Force is sufficient for all the spiritual work in the world. God only needs the instruments for his use. His instruments can remake the world.

Prayer for the Day

*I pray that I may be an instrument
of the Divine Power.*

AA Thought for the Day

 People generally make two mistakes about alcoholism. One mistake is that it can be cured by physical treatment only. The other mistake is that it can be cured by willpower only. Most alcoholics have tried both of these ways and have found that they don't work. But we members of AA have found a way to deal with alcoholism. *Have I gotten over my obsession by following the AA program?*

Meditation for the Day

I will keep calm in the face of disturbance, will keep that deep, inner calm through all the experiences of the day. In the rush of work and worry, the deep, inner silence is necessary to keep me on an even keel.

Prayer for the Day

I pray that I may be still and commune with God. I pray that I may learn patience, humility, and peace.

AA Thought for the Day

Alcohol is poison to the alcoholic. *Poison* is not too strong a word, because alcoholism leads eventually to the death of the alcoholic. *Do I know that since I'm an alcoholic all liquor is poison to me?*

Meditation for the Day

I must somehow find the means of coming nearer to God. That is what really matters. I must somehow seek the true bread of life, which is communion with him.

Prayer for the Day

I pray that I may meet God in quiet communion. I pray that I may partake of the soul-food that God has provided for me.

AA Thought for the Day

 After we became alcoholics, alcohol poisoned our love for family and friends, it poisoned our ambition, it poisoned our self-respect. It poisoned our whole lives, until we met AA. We will keep training our minds never even to think of liquor again in any way except as a poison. *Do I believe that liquor will poison my life if I ever touch it again?*

Meditation for the Day

It is not the passionate appeal that gains God's attention as much as the quiet placing of difficulty and worry in the Divine Hands. So I will trust God like a child who places a tangled skein of wool in the hands of a loving parent to unravel. I please God more by my unquestioning confidence than by imploring him for help.

Prayer for the Day

I pray that I may put all my difficulties in God's hands and leave them there. I pray that I may fully trust God to take care of them.

AA Thought for the Day

 Many things we do in AA are in preparation for that crucial moment when, walking down the street on a nice sunshiny day, the idea of having a cool drink pops into our minds. If we've trained our minds so that we're well prepared for that crucial moment, we won't take that first drink. *In preparation for that crucial moment when I'll be tempted, will I keep in mind the fact that liquor is my enemy?*

Meditation for the Day

How many of the world's prayers have gone unanswered because those who prayed did not endure to the end? They thought that they must act for themselves, that God was not going to guide them. If I endure, God will unlock those secret spiritual treasures.

Prayer for the Day

I pray that I may never doubt the power of God and try to take things into my own hands.

AA Thought for the Day

We used to have a lot of fun drinking. Practically all the fun we had was connected with drinking. But the time came when liquor became our enemy. And since we realize that liquor is now our enemy, our main business is keeping sober. Any other activity is secondary to the business of keeping sober. *Do I realize that my main business is keeping sober?*

Meditation for the Day

I can depend on God to supply me with all the power I need to face any situation, provided that I sincerely believe in that power and honestly ask for it.

Prayer for the Day

I pray that I may ask only for faith and strength to meet any situation.

AA Thought for the Day

We go to AA meetings because it helps us in our business of keeping sober. And we try to help other alcoholics when we can, because that's part of the business of keeping sober. We also have a partner in this business and that's God. We pray to him every day to help us to stay sober. *Am I in the business of keeping sober?*

Meditation for the Day

I will be more afraid of spirit unrest, of soul disturbance, of any ruffling of the mind, than of earthquake or fire. When I feel the calm of my spirit has been broken by emotional upset, then I must steal away alone with God.

Prayer for the Day

*I pray that I may keep a calm spirit
and a steady heart.*

AA Thought for the Day

 Now we can take an inventory of the good things that have come to us through AA. To begin with, we're sober today. That's the biggest asset on any alcoholic's books. Everything else depends on that. *Do I realize that my job, my family, and my real friends are dependent upon my sobriety?*

Meditation for the Day

I must trust God to the best of my ability. This lesson has to be learned. My doubts and fears continually drive me back into the wilderness. Doubts lead me astray, because I am not trusting God. I must trust God's love. It will never fail me.

Prayer for the Day

I pray that I may live the way God wants me to live. I pray that I may get into that stream of goodness in the world.

AA Thought for the Day

 Besides our jobs, our families, our friends, and our sobriety, we have something else that many of us found through AA. That's faith in a Power greater than ourselves, to which we can turn for help. We have these things because we're sober. *Do I make one resolution every day of my life—to stay sober?*

Meditation for the Day

I must take my fill of joy in the spring. Live outdoors whenever possible. Sun and air are nature's great healing forces. But I must never forget that the real healing of the spirit comes from within, from the close, loving contact of my spirit with God's spirit.

Prayer for the Day

*I pray that I may learn to live
the abundant life.*

AA Thought for the Day

 When we came to our first AA meeting, we looked up at the wall at the end of the room and saw the sign, "But for the grace of God." We heard speakers tell how they had come to depend on a Power greater than themselves. *Am I depending on the grace of God to help me stay sober?*

Meditation for the Day

If I share my love, my joy, my happiness, my time, my food, my money gladly with all; if I give out all the love I can with a glad, free heart and hand; if I do all I can for others, then back will come countless stores of blessings. Sharing draws others to me. I take all who come as sent by God and give them a royal welcome.

Prayer for the Day

I pray that I may make each visitor desire to return.

AA Thought for the Day

Some people find it difficult to believe in a Power greater than themselves. We can all agree that alcohol is a power greater than ourselves. We were helpless before the power of alcohol. *Do I remember the things that happened to me because of the power of alcohol?*

Meditation for the Day

Faith, fellowship, and service are cures for most of the ills of the world. There is nothing in the field of personal relationships that they cannot do.

Prayer for the Day

I pray that I may do my share
in making a better world.

AA Thought for the Day

 When we came into AA, we came to believe in a Power greater than ourselves to whom we can turn for help. Each morning we have a quiet time. We ask God for the power to stay sober for the next twenty-four hours. And each night we thank him for helping us to keep sober that day. *Do I believe that each person I see in AA is a demonstration of the power of God to change a human being from a drunkard to a sober person?*

Meditation for the Day

I should pray for faith as a thirsty person prays for water in a desert. There is nothing lacking in my life because, really, all I need is mine, only I lack the faith to know it.

Prayer for the Day

I pray that I may know that God's power is always available.

AA Thought for the Day

 When we came into AA, the first thing we did was to admit that we couldn't do anything about our drinking. We never could decide whether or not to take a drink. We always took the drink. And since we couldn't do anything about it ourselves, we put our whole drinking problem into the hands of God. And we have nothing more to do about it, except to trust God to take care of the problem for us. *Have I done this honestly and fully?*

Meditation for the Day

This is the time for my spirit to touch the spirit of God. I know that the feeling of the spirit-touch is more important than all the sensations of material things. God's touch is a potent healer.

Prayer for the Day

I pray that the fever of resentment, worry, and fear may melt into nothingness. I pray that health, joy, peace, and serenity may take its place.

AA Thought for the Day

 We should be free from alcohol for good. It's out of our hands and in the hands of God, so we don't need to worry about it or even think about it anymore. But if we haven't done this honestly and fully, the chances are that it will become our problem again. *Do I trust God to take care of the problem for me?*

Meditation for the Day

No work is of value without preparation. Every spiritual work must have behind it much spiritual preparation. If I cut short my times of prayer and times of spiritual preparation, my hours of work may be profitless.

Prayer for the Day

I pray that I may spend more time
alone with God.

AA Thought for the Day

Getting sober was a long and painful journey, but we can truthfully say it was worth it. We know now that all we've been through led us to AA and was part of our spiritual journey. We found in AA what we had been vainly seeking in the bottle. *Do I turn to my Higher Power to sustain me as I continue the spiritual journey that brought me to AA?*

Meditation for the Day

As I continue on my spiritual journey, I will seek and follow Divine Guidance and know there is always a place prepared for me. My only responsibility is to accept God's guidance and follow the highest principles in all my affairs.

Prayer for the Day

I pray to trust that I am always doing the right thing and am in the right place when my Higher Power is leading me.

MARCH

AA Thought for the Day

When we find ourselves thinking about taking a drink, we say to ourselves, *Don't reach out and take that problem back. You've given it to God and there's nothing you can do about it.* So we forget about the drink. If we let God have it and keep it for good, we'll stay sober. *Have I determined not to take the drinking problem back to myself?*

Meditation for the Day

Constant effort is necessary if I am to grow spiritually and develop my spiritual life. I must keep the spiritual rules persistently, perseveringly, lovingly, patiently, and hopefully.

Prayer for the Day

I pray that God's spirit may be everything to my soul. I pray that God's spirit may grow within me.

AA Thought for the Day

 Over a period of drinking years, we've proved to ourselves and to everybody else that we can't stop drinking by our own willpower. You really get this program when you get down on your knees and surrender yourself to God, as you understand him. Surrender means putting your life into God's hands. *Have I made a promise to God that I will try to live the way he wants me to live?*

Meditation for the Day

Spirit-power comes from communication with God in prayer and times of quiet meditation. I must constantly seek spirit-communication with God. Many people do not realize the power that can come to them from direct spirit-communication.

Prayer for the Day

I pray that I may feel that God's power is mine.

AA Thought for the Day

After we've made a surrender, the drinking problem is out of our hands and in the hands of God. The thing we have to do is to be sure that we never reach out and take the problem back into our own hands. Whenever we're tempted to take a drink we say a little prayer to God. *Am I going to keep my bargain with God?*

Meditation for the Day

My sense of failure is a sure sign that I am growing. In sloth—physical, mental, or spiritual—there is no sense of failure or discomfort. With struggle and effort, I am conscious not of strength but of weakness. But in the struggle I can always rely on the power of God to help me.

Prayer for the Day

*I pray that I may see signs of my growth
in the new life.*

AA Thought for the Day

 Having surrendered our lives to God and having put our drinking problem in his hands doesn't mean that we'll never be tempted to drink. So we must build up strength for the time when temptation will come. We start the day in quiet time. We read and pray and get our minds in the right mood for the day. *Am I trying to live the way God wants me to live?*

Meditation for the Day

The elimination of selfishness is the key to happiness and can only be accomplished with God's help. I start out with a spark of the Divine Spirit but a large amount of selfishness. I can become more unselfish and develop my spirituality until it becomes the most important thing in my life.

Prayer for the Day

I pray that I may take the right path every day.

AA Thought for the Day

 Sometimes we try too hard to get this program. It is better to relax and accept it. It will be given to us, with no effort on our part. We must say to God, "Here am I and here are all my troubles. I've made a mess of things and can't do anything about it. You take me and all my troubles and do anything you want with me." *Do I believe that the grace of God can do for me what I could never do for myself?*

Meditation for the Day

Many are our fears. Fear cannot exist where true love is or where faith abides. So I must have no fear. Fear is evil, but "perfect love casts out all fear."

Prayer for the Day

I pray that I may cast all fear out of my life.

AA Thought for the Day

 We surrender our lives to God and ask him for help. When he knows that we're ready, he gives us by his grace the free gift of sobriety. And we can't take any credit for having stopped drinking, because we didn't do it by our own willpower. *Do I believe that God has made me a free gift of the strength to stay sober?*

Meditation for the Day

I must work for God, with God, and through God's help. I have to rely on God's power, and anything I accomplish is through his help.

Prayer for the Day

I pray that I may work for God
and with God.

AA Thought for the Day

 There are two important things we have to do if we want to get sober and stay sober. First, having admitted that we're helpless before alcohol, we have to turn our alcoholic problem over to God and trust him to take care of it for us. Second, we must cooperate with him by doing something about it ourselves. *Am I doing these two things?*

Meditation for the Day

I must prepare myself by doing each day what I can to develop spiritually and to help others to do so. I must want God's will for me above all else. I must not expect to have what I am not prepared for.

Prayer for the Day

I pray that I may really try to do God's will in all my affairs.

AA Thought for the Day

 We must go to AA meetings regularly. We must change from alcoholic thinking to sober thinking. We must try to help other alcoholics. We must cooperate with God by spending at least as much time and energy on the AA program as we did on drinking. *Have I turned my alcoholic problem over to God, and am I cooperating with him?*

Meditation for the Day

The joy of true fellowship shall be mine in full measure. There will come back a wonderful joy if I share in fellowship now. Fellowship among spiritually minded people is the embodiment of God's purpose for this world.

Prayer for the Day

I pray that I may sense his presence in spiritual fellowship with his children.

AA Thought for the Day

 Our faith is apt to be weak, and so we have to strengthen and build up this faith. We do this by going to meetings and listening to others tell how they have found all the strength they need to overcome drinking. *Is my faith being strengthened by this personal witness of other alcoholics?*

Meditation for the Day

It is the quality of my life that determines its value. The most valuable life is one of honesty, purity, unselfishness, and love.

Prayer for the Day

I pray that I may be honest, pure, unselfish, and loving.

AA Thought for the Day

 We strengthen our faith by working with other alcoholics and finding that we can do nothing ourselves to help them, except to tell them our own story of how we found the way out. If the other person is helped, it's by the grace of God. We also strengthen our faith by having quiet times every morning. *Do I ask God in this quiet time for the strength to stay sober this day?*

Meditation for the Day

I must sever all connections with the material world when I wish to hold communion with the Great Spirit of the universe. I have to hush my mind and bid all my senses be still.

Prayer for the Day

I pray that I may get my spirit in tune
with the Spirit of the universe.

AA Thought for the Day

 By having quiet times each morning, we come to depend on God's help during the day, especially if we are tempted to take a drink. And we can honestly thank him each night for the strength he has given us. So our faith is strengthened. *Have I turned my drinking problem entirely over to God, without reservations?*

Meditation for the Day

It seems that when God wants to express to people what he is like, he makes a very beautiful character. I can think of a personality as God's expression of character attributes and look for beauty of character in those around me.

Prayer for the Day

I pray that I may look at great souls until their beauty of character becomes a part of my soul.

AA Thought for the Day

 The prodigal son "took his journey into a far country, and there he squandered his property in loose living. When he came to himself, he said, 'I will arise and go to my father.'" That's what we do in AA. We come to ourselves. Our alcoholic self is not our real self. Our sane, sober, respectable self is our real self. That's why we alcoholics are so happy in AA. *Have I come to myself?*

Meditation for the Day

Simplicity is the keynote of a good life. I can choose the simple things always. Every difficulty can be either solved or ignored and something better substituted for it. Appreciate the simple things. My standard must never be the world's standard of wealth and power.

Prayer for the Day

I pray that I may keep my life uncomplicated and free.

AA Thought for the Day

 We turn to God, our Father, for help, just as the prodigal son arose and went to his father. At the end of the story, the father of the prodigal son says, "My son was dead and is alive again; he was lost, and is found." We alcoholics who have found sobriety in AA were certainly dead and are alive again. We were lost and are found. *Am I alive again?*

Meditation for the Day

I gently breathe in God's spirit, that spirit which, if not kept out by selfishness, will enable me to do good works. I can become a channel for God's spirit which will flow through me and into the lives of others. If my spirit is in harmony with God's spirit, there is no limit to what I can do in the realm of human relationships.

Prayer for the Day

I pray that God's spirit may flow through me into the lives of others.

AA Thought for the Day

 Can we get well? If we mean, "Can we ever drink normally again?" the answer is no. But if we mean, "Can we stay sober?" the answer is definitely yes. We can get well by turning our drinking problems over to a Power greater than ourselves and by asking that Power each morning to give us the strength to stay sober for the next twenty-four hours. *Am I faithfully following the AA program?*

Meditation for the Day

I persevere in all that God's guidance moves me to do. If I look back over God's guidance, I will see that his leading has been very gradual and that only as I have carried out his wishes, as far as I can understand them, has God been able to give me more clear and definite leading.

Prayer for the Day

*I pray that I may persevere in doing
what seems right.*

AA Thought for the Day

We alcoholics were on a merry-go-round, going round and round, and we couldn't get off. That merry-go-round is a kind of hell on earth. In AA I got off that merry-go-round by learning to stay sober. *Am I off the merry-go-round of drinking for good?*

Meditation for the Day

I must remember that in spiritual matters I am only an instrument. It is not for me to decide how or when I am to act. It is up to me to make myself fit to do God's work. All that hinders my spiritual activity must be eliminated.

Prayer for the Day

I pray that my selfishness will not hinder my progress in spiritual matters.

AA Thought for the Day

Before we decide to quit drinking, most of us have to come up against a blank wall. We see that we're licked, that we have to quit. But we don't know which way to turn for help. AA opens the door that leads to sobriety by encouraging us to honestly admit that we're alcoholics. *Have I gone through that door to sobriety?*

Meditation for the Day

I must have a singleness of purpose to do my part in God's work. I must not let material distractions interfere with my job of improving personal relationships.

Prayer for the Day

I pray that I may concentrate on doing
what I can do best.

AA Thought for the Day

By having regular meetings so that we can associate with other alcoholics, by encouraging us to tell the story of our own sad experiences with alcohol, and by showing us how to help other alcoholics, AA keeps us sober. *Am I going to step back through that door in the wall to my old helpless, hopeless, drunken life?*

Meditation for the Day

I withdraw into the calm of communion with God. I rest in that calm and peace. When the soul finds its home of rest in God, then real life begins.

Prayer for the Day

I pray that I may keep serene
at the center of my being.

AA Thought for the Day

 When we face the fact that we must spend the rest of our lives without liquor, it often seems like an impossibility to us. So AA tells us to forget about the future and take it one day at a time. All we really have is now. As the saying goes, "Yesterday is gone, forget it; tomorrow never comes, don't worry; today is here, get busy." When tomorrow gets here, it will be today. *Am I living one day at a time?*

Meditation for the Day

Persistence is necessary if I am to advance in spiritual things. By persistent prayer, persistent, firm, and simple trust, I achieve the treasures of the spirit.

Prayer for the Day

I pray that I may persistently carry out my spiritual exercises every day.

AA Thought for the Day

Remorse is terrible mental punishment: ashamed of ourselves for the things we've said and done, afraid to face people because of what they might think of us, afraid of the consequences of what we did when we were drunk. In AA we forget about the past. *Do I believe that God has forgiven me for everything I've done in the past, no matter how bad it was, provided I'm honestly trying to do the right thing today?*

Meditation for the Day

God's spirit is all around me all day long. I have no thoughts, no plans, no impulses, no emotions that he does not know about. I can hide nothing from him. I cannot make my conduct conform only to that of the world and cannot depend on the approval or disapproval of others.

Prayer for the Day

I pray that I may realize God's presence constantly all through the day.

AA Thought for the Day

When we were drinking, we used to worry about the future. Worry is terrible mental punishment. We can see ourselves slipping, getting worse and worse, and we wonder what the finish will be. Sometimes we get so discouraged in thinking about the future that we toy with the idea of suicide. *In AA, have I stopped worrying about the future?*

Meditation for the Day

Functioning on a material plane alone takes me away from God. I must also try to function on a spiritual plane. I must try to obey God as I would expect a faithful, willing servant to carry out directions.

Prayer for the Day

I pray that the flow of God's spirit may come to me through many channels.

AA Thought for the Day

 In AA we forget about the future. We know from experience that as time goes on, the future takes care of itself. Everything works out well, as long as we stay sober. All we need to think about is today. *Do I know that this day is all I have and that with God's help I can stay sober today?*

Meditation for the Day

All is fundamentally well. That does not mean that all is well on the surface of things. But it does mean that God's in his heaven and that he has a purpose for the world, which will eventually work out when enough human beings are willing to follow his way.

Prayer for the Day

*I pray that God may be with me
in my journey through the world.*

AA Thought for the Day

 We're all looking for the power to overcome drinking. When we alcoholics come into AA, our first question is, "How do I get the strength to quit?" At first it seems to us that we will never get the necessary strength. We see older members who have found the power we are looking for, but we don't know the process by which they got it. This necessary strength comes in many ways. *Have I found all the strength I need?*

Meditation for the Day

I receive the best spiritual supply when I want it to pass on to other people. I get it largely by giving it away. God gives me strength as I pass it on to another person.

Prayer for the Day

*I pray that I may use the power I receive
to help others.*

AA Thought for the Day

Strength comes from the fellowship we find when we come into AA. Just being with people who have found the way out gives us a feeling of security. We listen to the speakers and we absorb the atmosphere of confidence and hope that we find in the place. *Am I receiving strength from the fellowship with other AA members?*

Meditation for the Day

God is with me, to bless and help me. His spirit is all around me. All power is God's. I say that to myself often and steadily. I say that until my heart sings with joy for the safety and personal power that it means to me.

Prayer for the Day

I pray that with strength from God I may lead an abundant life.

AA Thought for the Day

Strength comes from honestly telling our own experiences with drinking. In religion, they call it confession. We call it witnessing, or sharing. We give a personal witness, we share our past experiences, the troubles we got into. This personal witness lets out the things we had kept hidden, brings them out into the open, and we find release and strength. *Am I receiving strength from my personal witnessing?*

Meditation for the Day

I cannot fully understand the universe. I can never know all things, nor am I made to know them. Much of my life must be taken on faith.

Prayer for the Day

I pray that my faith may be based on my own experience of the power of God in my life.

AA Thought for the Day

 We hear other alcoholics talk about a Higher Power, and we begin to get the idea ourselves. We try praying in a quiet time each morning and we begin to feel stronger, as though our prayers were heard. So we gradually come to believe there must be a Power in the world outside ourselves, which is stronger than us and to which we can turn for help. *Am I receiving strength from my faith in a Higher Power?*

Meditation for the Day

Spiritual development is achieved by daily persistence in living the way I believe God wants me to live. Like the wearing away of a stone by steady drops of water, so will my daily persistence wear away all of the difficulties and gain spiritual success for me. I go forward boldly and unafraid. God will help and strengthen me.

Prayer for the Day

I pray that I may persist day by day in gaining spiritual experience. I pray that I may make this a lifetime work.

AA Thought for the Day

 Strength comes from working with other alcoholics. When we are trying to help a new prospect with the program, we are building up our own strength at the same time. We see the other person in the condition we might be in ourselves and that makes our resolve to stay sober stronger than ever. Often, we help ourselves more than the other person. *Am I receiving strength from working with others?*

Meditation for the Day

I can experience the power of God's spirit through my faith. Faith is the bridge between us, which I can take or not, as I will. I must make the choice.

Prayer for the Day

*I pray that I may decide to cross
the bridge of faith.*

AA Thought for the Day

We get the power to overcome drinking through the fellowship of other alcoholics who have found the way out. We get power by honestly sharing our past experiences, by having a personal witness. We get power by coming to believe in a Higher Power. We get power by working with other alcoholics. *Am I ready and willing to accept this power and work for it?*

Meditation for the Day

One who conquers oneself is greater than one who conquers a city. Material things have no permanence. But God's spirit is eternal.

Prayer for the Day

I pray that I may open myself
to the power of God's spirit.

AA Thought for the Day

 When we come into an AA meeting, we're not just coming into a meeting, we're coming into a new life. It is easy to notice the change we see in people after they've been in AA for a while. We need to remind ourselves to take an inventory of ourselves, to see whether we have changed and, if so, in what way. *Am I still all "get" and no "give"?*

Meditation for the Day

There are two things that I must have if I am going to change my way of life. One is faith in the fundamental goodness and purpose in the universe. The other is obedience: that is, living according to my faith, living each day as I believe that God wants me to live, with gratitude, humility, honesty, purity, unselfishness, and love.

Prayer for the Day

I pray that I may have more faith and obedience.

AA Thought for the Day

Before we met AA, we were very dishonest. We lied constantly. We were dishonest with ourselves, as well as with other people. We would never face ourselves as we really were or admit when we were wrong. We pretended to ourselves that we were as good as the next person, although we suspected we weren't. *Am I now really honest?*

Meditation for the Day

I can go forth from my secret times of communion with God to the work of the world. To get the spiritual strength I need, my inner life must be lived apart from the world. Nothing in the world should seriously upset me, as long as my inner life is lived with God.

Prayer for the Day

I pray that I may live my inner life with God.
I pray that nothing will invade or destroy
that secret place of peace.

AA Thought for the Day

 Before we met AA, we were very unloving. We paid very little attention to our families. We lived as if we were on our own and didn't even bother to share our lives with them. We failed to develop close friendships and only hung around people who wanted to party. We couldn't be bothered by anyone else. *Have I gotten over loving nobody but myself?*

Meditation for the Day

I will be calm, true, and quiet. I will not get emotionally upset by anything that happens around me. I feel a deep, inner security in the goodness and purpose in the universe. I do not let myself slip back into the old ways of reacting. I accept criticism as well as I accept praise. Only God can judge the real me.

Prayer for the Day

*I pray that I will not be upset
by the judgment of others.*

AA Thought for the Day

 Since we've been in AA, have we made a start toward being more un- selfish? Do we no longer want our own way in everything? When things go wrong and we can't have what we want, do we no longer sulk? Are we trying not to waste money on ourselves? And does it make us happy to see our loved ones get enough atten- tion from us? *Am I trying not to be all "get" and no "give"?*

Meditation for the Day

Each day is a day of steady progress forward, if I make it so. I may not see it, but God does. God judges by the heart. I want him to see in my heart a simple desire always to do his will.

Prayer for the Day

*I pray that I may advance each day
in spite of my stumbling feet.*

APRIL

AA Thought for the Day

 Since we've been in AA, have we made a start toward becoming more honest? Do we no longer have to lie to our loved ones? Do we try to have meals on time, do we try to earn what we make at work, do we do the best that we can? *Am I beginning to find out what it means to be alive and to face the world honestly and without fear?*

Meditation for the Day

God is all around me. His spirit pervades the universe. And yet I often do not let his spirit in. I try to get along without his help, and I make a mess of my life. I can do nothing of any value without God's help.

Prayer for the Day

I pray that I may let God run my life.

AA Thought for the Day

 Since we've been in AA, have we made a start toward becoming more loving to our families and friends? Are we grateful to our families for having put up with us? Do we feel that the friends we've found in AA are real friends? *Do I really care now about other people?*

Meditation for the Day

Changed by God's grace, I shed one garment of the spirit for a better one. In time, I throw that one aside for a better one. And so from character to character, I am gradually transformed.

Prayer for the Day

I pray that each acceptance of a challenge may make me grow into a better person.

AA Thought for the Day

 When we were drinking, we were absolutely selfish. We thought of ourselves first, last, and always. The universe revolved around us at the center. To quit drinking was impossible. We couldn't see beyond ourselves and our need for another drink. *Can I now look out and beyond my own selfishness?*

Meditation for the Day

The first quality of greatness is service. God is the greatest servant of all, because he is always waiting for me to call on him to help me in all good endeavors. A life of service is the finest life I can live. I am here on earth to serve others. That is the beginning and the end of my real worth.

Prayer for the Day

I pray that I may serve God and others.

AA Thought for the Day

 When we came into AA, we found people who had been through the same things we had been through. But now they were thinking more about how they could help others than they were about themselves. By coming to meetings and associating with them, we began to think a little less about ourselves and a little more about other people. *Am I now depending less on myself and more on God?*

Meditation for the Day

I cannot help others unless I understand the person I am trying to help. When I see another's weaknesses, I do not confront the person with them. I share my own weaknesses, sins, and temptations and let other people find their own convictions.

Prayer for the Day

I pray that I may serve as a channel for God's power to come into the lives of others.

AA Thought for the Day

 People often ask what makes the AA program work. One of the answers is that AA works because it gets us away from ourselves as the center of the universe. And it teaches us to rely more on the fellowship of others and on strength from God. *Are these things keeping me sober?*

Meditation for the Day

God is the great interpreter of one human personality to another. Each personality is so different. God alone understands perfectly the language of each and can interpret between the two. Here I find the miracles of change and the true interpretation of life.

Prayer for the Day

I pray that I may be in the right relationship to God.

AA Thought for the Day

All alcoholics have personality problems. We drink to escape from life, to counteract feelings of loneliness or inferiority, or because of some emotional conflict within so that we cannot adjust ourselves to life. As alcoholics, we cannot stop drinking unless we find a way to solve our personality problems. *Was my personality problem ever solved by going on the wagon or taking the pledge?*

Meditation for the Day

As I unclasp my hold on material things, the tide of peace and serenity flows in. I do not hold on to earth's treasures so firmly that my hands are too occupied to clasp God's hands as he holds them out to me in love.

Prayer for the Day

I pray that I may be willing to relinquish my hold on material things and receive them back from God.

AA Thought for the Day

 In AA alcoholics find a way to solve personality problems. We do this by recovering three things. First, we recover our personal integrity. We get honest with ourselves and with other people. We take a personal inventory of ourselves to see where we really stand. *Have I recovered my integrity?*

Meditation for the Day

When trouble comes, I do not say, "Why should this happen to me?" If I leave myself out of the picture and think of other people and their troubles, I will forget about my own. After awhile, it will not matter so much what happens to me.

Prayer for the Day

I pray that I will not be thrown off the track by letting the old selfishness creep back into my life.

AA Thought for the Day

 Second, as alcoholics we recover faith in a Power greater than ourselves. We admit that we're helpless by ourselves and we call on that Higher Power for help. We surrender our lives to God, as we understand him. We put our drinking problem in God's hands and leave it there. *Have I recovered my faith?*

Meditation for the Day

I must make a stand for God. Believers in God are considered by some as peculiar people. I must even be willing to be deemed a fool for the sake of my faith. I can be known by the marks that distinguish a believer in God. These are honesty, purity, unselfishness, love, gratitude, and humility.

Prayer for the Day

I pray that I will not be turned aside by the skepticism and cynicism of unbelievers.

AA Thought for the Day

Third, alcoholics recover a proper relationship with other people. We think
less about ourselves and more about
others. We try to help other alcoholics. We make new friends so that we're no
longer lonely. We try to live a life of service instead of selfishness. *Is my drinking problem
solved as long as my personality problem is
solved?*

Meditation for the Day

All that depresses me, all that I fear, is really
powerless to harm me. These things are but
phantoms. So I arise from earth's bonds, from
depression, distrust, fear, and all that hinders
a new life. I arise to beauty, joy, peace, and
work inspired by love.

Prayer for the Day

*I pray that I will let God live in me
as I work for him.*

AA Thought for the Day

When we came into AA, we came into a new world. A sober world. A world of sobriety, peace, serenity, and happiness. But we know that if we take just one drink, we'll go right back into that old world. That alcoholic world. That world of drunkenness, conflict, and misery. *Do I want to go back to that alcoholic world?*

Meditation for the Day

God can only dwell with the humble and the obedient. Obedience to God's will is the key unlocking the door to God's kingdom. I cannot obey God to the best of my ability without in time realizing God's love and responding to that love. Where God's spirit is, there is my home. There is heaven for me.

Prayer for the Day

*I pray that I may obey God's guidance
to the best of my ability.*

AA Thought for the Day

In that alcoholic world, one drink always leads to another and we can't stop till we're paralyzed. And the next morning it begins all over again. We're always in a mess. We're on the merry-go-round and we can't get off. We're in a squirrel cage and we can't get out. *Am I convinced that the alcoholic world is not a pleasant place for me to live?*

Meditation for the Day

I must learn to accept self-discipline, even if the discipline keeps me separated from some people who are without discipline. I will try to live the way I believe God wants me to live, no matter what others say.

Prayer for the Day

I pray that I may be an example to others
of a better way of living.

AA Thought for the Day

This sober world is a pleasant place for an alcoholic to live. Once we've gotten out of our alcoholic fog, we find that the world looks good. We find real friends in AA. We feel good in the morning. We eat a good breakfast, and we do a good day's work at home or at school. And our families welcome us. *Am I convinced that this sober world is a pleasant place for an alcoholic to live?*

Meditation for the Day

My need is God's opportunity. First I must recognize my need. Next comes faith in the power of God's spirit, available to me to meet that need. An expression of faith is all God needs to manifest his power in my life.

Prayer for the Day

I pray that I may have faith that God will meet my needs, in the way that is best for me.

AA Thought for the Day

 Having found our way into this new world by the grace of God and the help of AA, are we going to take that first drink, when we know that just one drink will change our whole world? Or are we going to hang on to the happiness of this sober world? Is there any doubt about the answer? *With God's help, am I going to hang on to AA with both hands?*

Meditation for the Day

I will try to make the world better and happier by my presence in it. I will be gentle with all people. I will always pray to God to act as interpreter between me and a person in need.

Prayer for the Day

*I pray that I may depend on God for the strength
I need to help me do my part in making
the world a better place.*

AA Thought for the Day

 A police captain once told about certain cases he had come across in his police work. The cause of the tragedy in each case was drunkenness. He told his audience about a man who got into an argument with his wife while he was drunk and beat her to death. Then he went out and drank some more. The police captain also told about a woman who got too near the edge of an old quarry hole when she was drunk and fell 150 feet to her death. *When I read or hear these stories, do I think about our motto, "But for the grace of God"?*

Meditation for the Day

I must keep balance by keeping spiritual things at the center of my life. Then I will be at peace amid the distractions of everyday living.

Prayer for the Day

I pray that I will dwell with God at the center of my life.

AA Thought for the Day

 We will never know what might have happened to us when we were drunk. We usually thought, *That couldn't happen to me.* But any one of us could have killed somebody or have been killed ourselves, if we were drunk enough. But fear of these things never kept us from drinking. *Do I believe that in AA we have something more effective than fear?*

Meditation for the Day

I must keep calm. I must go back into the silence of communion with God to recover this calm when it is lost even for one moment. I will accomplish more by this calmness than by all the activities of a long day. At all cost I will keep calm.

Prayer for the Day

*I pray that I may keep myself in that state
of calmness that comes from faith in God's purpose
for the world.*

AA Thought for the Day

 In AA we have insurance. Our faith in God is a kind of insurance against the terrible things that might happen to us if we ever drink again. *Am I paying my AA insurance premiums regularly?*

Meditation for the Day

I must try to love all humanity. Love comes from thinking of every person as my brother or sister, because they are children of God. Love means no severe judging, no resentments, no malicious gossip, and no destructive criticism. It means patience, understanding, compassion, and helpfulness.

Prayer for the Day

*I pray that I will have love
for all of God's children.*

AA Thought for the Day

 Every time we go to an AA meeting, every time we say the Lord's Prayer, every time we have a quiet time before breakfast, we're paying a premium on our insurance against taking that first drink. And every time we help another alcoholic, we're making a large payment on our drink insurance. *Am I building up an endowment in serenity, peace, and happiness that will put me on easy street for the rest of my life?*

Meditation for the Day

The persistent recognition of God's spirit in all of my personal relationships, the evidence in support of God's guidance, the numberless instances in which seeming chance or wonderful coincidence can be traced to God's purpose in my life—all these things gradually engender a feeling of wonder, humility, and gratitude to God.

Prayer for the Day

I pray that I will find confirmation of my life in the good things that have come into my life.

AA Thought for the Day

 As we look back over our drinking careers, have we learned that we take out of life what we put into it? When we put drinking into our lives, did we take out a lot of bad things? *When I put drinking into my life, was almost everything I took out bad?*

Meditation for the Day

I should strive for a friendliness and helpfulness that will affect all who come near me. I must send no one away without a word of cheer, a feeling that I really care about each person.

Prayer for the Day

*I pray that I may warmly welcome all
who come to me for help.*

AA Thought for the Day

 Since we've been putting sobriety into our lives, we feel good. We feel right with the world. As long as we put sobriety into our lives, we feel a kind of quiet satisfaction. *Am I getting satisfaction out of living a sober life?*

Meditation for the Day

It is a glorious way—the upward way. There are wonderful discoveries in the realm of the spirit. There are tender intimacies in the quiet times of communion with God. There is an amazing, almost incomprehensible understanding of the other person. You can have all the strength you need from that Higher Power.

Prayer for the Day

I pray that I will keep going forward to the more abundant life.

AA Thought for the Day

 The satisfaction we get out of living a sober life is made up of a lot of little things, but they add up to a satisfactory and happy life. Don't worry about what life will be like without liquor. Just hang in there and a lot of good things will happen to us. *Is my life becoming really worth living?*

Meditation for the Day

There are two paths, one up and one down. I have been given free will to choose either path. I am captain of my soul to this extent only. On the right path, I have all the power of God's spirit behind me.

Prayer for the Day

I pray that I will be in the stream of goodness, on the side of all good in the universe.

APRIL 21

AA Thought for the Day

 After we've been in AA for a while, we find out that if we're going to stay sober, we have to be humble. The people in AA who have achieved so-briety are humble. *Am I grateful and humble?*

Meditation for the Day

All the old sins and temptations must be laid in the grave and a new existence must rise from the ashes. Yesterday is gone. All my sins are forgiven if I am honestly trying to do God's will today.

Prayer for the Day

I pray that I will share in making the world a better place to live.

AA Thought for the Day

People believe in AA when they see it work. What they read in books or what they hear people say doesn't always convince them. But when they see a real honest-to-goodness change take place in a person, that's something they can believe. *Have I seen the change in people who come into AA?*

Meditation for the Day

Divine control and unquestioning obedience to God are the only conditions necessary for a spiritual life. Divine control means absolute faith and trust in God, a belief that God is the intelligence and the love that controls the universe. Unquestioning obedience to God means living each day the way I believe God wants me to live, constantly seeking the guidance of God in every situation and being willing to do the right thing at all times.

Prayer for the Day

I pray that I will be always ready to serve God.

AA Thought for the Day

People keep coming into AA, licked by alcohol, often given up by doctors as hopeless cases, they themselves admitting they're helpless to stop drinking. When we see them get sober and stay sober over a period of months and years, we know that AA works. *Am I convinced that a Higher Power can help me to change?*

Meditation for the Day

Cooperation with God is the great necessity for my life. All else follows naturally. Cooperation with God is the result of my consciousness of his presence. Guidance is bound to come to me as I live more and more with God. I must have many quiet times when I ask not so much to be shown and led by God, as to feel and realize his presence.

Prayer for the Day

I pray that God will supply me with strength and show me the direction in which he wants me to grow.

AA Thought for the Day

 It's been proved that we alcoholics can't get sober by our willpower. We've failed again and again. Therefore there must be a Higher Power that helps us. Pray to God every morning for the strength to stay sober today. We know that power is there because it never fails to help us. *Do I believe that AA works through the grace of God?*

Meditation for the Day

Once I am "born of the spirit," that is my life's breath. Within me is the life of life, so that I can never perish—the life that down the ages has kept God's children through peril, adversity, and sorrow.

Prayer for the Day

I pray that my life may become centered in God more than in self. I pray that my will may be directed toward doing his will.

AA Thought for the Day

 We don't believe that AA works because we read it in a book or because we hear people say so. We believe it because we see people getting sober and staying sober. *Do I see AA work every day?*

Meditation for the Day

I try saying, "God bless her (or him)" of anyone who is not in harmony with me. I also say it of those who are in trouble through their own fault. I say it, willing that showers of blessings may fall upon them.

Prayer for the Day

I pray that I may accept God's blessing so that I will have harmony, beauty, joy, and happiness.

AA Thought for the Day

When we're drinking, we're submitting to a power greater than ourselves, liquor. Our own wills are no use against the power of liquor. In AA we submit to a Power, also greater than ourselves, which we call God. *Have I submitted myself to that Higher Power?*

Meditation for the Day

Ceaseless activity is not God's plan for my life. Times of withdrawal for renewed strength are always necessary. I wait for the faintest tremor of fear and stop all work, everything, and rest before God until I am strong again. I deal in the same way with all tired feelings.

Prayer for the Day

I pray that I will learn how to rest and listen, as well as how to work.

AA Thought for the Day

By submitting to God, we're released from the power of liquor. It has no more hold on us. We're also released from the things that were holding us down: pride, selfishness, and fear. And we're free to grow into a new life, which is so much better than the old life that there's no comparison. *Have I been released from the power of alcohol?*

Meditation for the Day

I know God by spiritual vision. I feel that he is beside me. I feel his presence. Spirit-consciousness replaces sight. Since I cannot see God, I have to perceive him by spiritual perception.

Prayer for the Day

I pray that I will have a consciousness of God's presence.

AA Thought for the Day

 We're so glad to be free from liquor that we do something about it. We come to meetings regularly. We go out and try to help other alcoholics. We pass on the good news whenever we get a chance. In a spirit of thankfulness to God, we get into action. *Have I gone into action?*

Meditation for the Day

God's eternal quest must be the tracking down of souls. If I join him in his quest, God leads me. I may not know which soul I will help, but I can leave all results to God and just go with him in his eternal quest for souls.

Prayer for the Day

I pray that I will offer God my helping hand.

AA Thought for the Day

 The AA program is one of faith, hope, and charity. It's a program of hope because when new members come into AA, they hear older members tell how they had been through the same kind of hell that they have and how they found the way out through AA. *Is hope still strong in me?*

Meditation for the Day

The rule of God's kingdom is perfect order, perfect harmony, perfect supply, perfect love, perfect honesty, perfect obedience. There is no discord in God's kingdom, only some things still unconquered in God's children. The difficulties of life are caused by disharmony in the individual person. God does not fail. People fail because they are out of harmony with him.

Prayer for the Day

*I pray that I will be in harmony with God
and with other people.*

AA Thought for the Day

 The AA program is one of faith because we find that we must have faith in a Power greater than ourselves if we are going to get sober. When we turn our drinking problem over to God and have faith that he can give us all the strength we need, then we have the drinking problem licked. *Is faith still strong in me?*

Meditation for the Day

I am a child of God, and as such, I am full of the promise of spiritual growth. There is a spark of the Divine in everyone. Each person has some of God's spirit that can be developed by spiritual exercise.

Prayer for the Day

*I pray that I may develop
the divine spark within me.*

MAY

AA Thought for the Day

 We may try to help somebody and think we have failed, but the seed we have planted may bear fruit some-time. We never know the results even a word of ours might have. But the main thing is to have charity for others, a real desire to help them, whether we succeed or not. *Do I have real charity?*

Meditation for the Day

Matter is thought. When eternal thought expresses itself within the framework of space and time, it becomes matter. My thoughts, within the box of space and time, cannot know anything firsthand, except material things. But I can deduce that outside the box of space and time is eternal thought, which I can call God.

Prayer for the Day

I pray that God's thoughts may work through my thoughts.

AA Thought for the Day

 In AA we often hear the slogan "Easy does it." Alcoholics always do everything to excess. We drink too much. We worry too much. We have too many resentments. We hurt ourselves physically and mentally by too much of everything. So when we come into AA, we have to learn to take it easy. *Have I learned to take it easy?*

Meditation for the Day

It is foolish to think that I can accomplish much in personal relationships without first preparing myself by being honest, pure, unselfish, and loving. I must choose the good and keep choosing it, before I am ready to be used by God to accomplish anything worthwhile. I will not be given the opportunities until I am ready for them.

Prayer for the Day

I pray that I may constantly prepare myself
for better things to come.

AA Thought for the Day

 AA teaches us to take it easy. We learn how to relax and to stop worrying about the past or the future, to give up our resentments and hates and tempers, to stop being critical of people, and to try to help them instead. *Is my motto going to be "Easy does it"?*

Meditation for the Day

The self in me cannot forgive injuries. The very thought of wrongs means that my self is in the foreground. Since the self cannot forgive, I must overcome my selfishness. It is a mistake for me even to think about these injuries. I must aim at overcoming myself in my daily life and then I will find there is nothing in me that remembers injury, because the only thing injured, my selfishness, is gone.

Prayer for the Day

I pray that my mind may be washed clean of all past hates and fears.

AA Thought for the Day

When we were drinking, we always tried to build ourselves up. We used to tell tall stories about ourselves. We told them so often that we half believe some of them now. We tried to build ourselves up because we knew deep down that we really didn't amount to anything. It was a kind of defense against our feelings of inferiority. *Do I still build myself up?*

Meditation for the Day

God thought about the universe and brought it into being. His thought brought me into being. I must keep my mind occupied with thoughts about God. I must think God's thought after him and meditate on the way he wants me to live.

Prayer for the Day

I pray that I may live as God wants me to live.

AA Thought for the Day

 Although we've been sober for quite a while, the old habit of building ourselves up is still with us. We still have a tendency to think too well of ourselves and to pretend to be more than we really are. *Am I always in danger of becoming conceited just because I'm sober?*

Meditation for the Day

I cannot experience the spiritual with my intellect. I can only do it by my own faith and spiritual faculties. I must think of God more with my heart than with my head. I am shut up in a box of space and time, but I can open a window in that box by faith.

Prayer for the Day

I pray that whatever is good I may have.
I pray that I may leave to God the choice
of what good will come to me.

AA Thought for the Day

 We've noticed that the ones who do the most for AA are not in the habit of boasting about it. The danger of building ourselves up too much is that, if we do, we're in danger of having a fall. Building ourselves up and drinking go together. So if we're going to stay sober, we've got to keep small. *Do I have the right perspective on myself?*

Meditation for the Day

The way sometimes seems long and weary. The weary and the heavy-laden, when they come to me, should be helped to find the rest that I have found. There is only one sure cure for world-weariness and that is turning to spiritual things.

Prayer for the Day

I pray that I may have the courage to help bring
about what the weary world needs
but does not know how to get.

AA Thought for the Day

 It's very important to keep in a grateful frame of mind, if we want to stay sober. We should be grateful that we're living in a day and age when alcoholics aren't treated as they often used to be treated before Alcoholics Anonymous was started. We have come into AA and found all the sympathy, understanding, and fellowship that we could ask for. There's no other group like AA in the world. *Am I grateful?*

Meditation for the Day

God takes my efforts for good and blesses them. God needs my efforts. I need God's blessing. Together, they mean spiritual success.

Prayer for the Day

I pray that I may have God's blessing and direction in all of my efforts for good.

AA Thought for the Day

We've found a happiness and contentment, that we had forgotten existed, by simply believing in God and trying to live the kind of lives that we know he wants us to live. As long as we stay grateful, we'll stay sober. *Am I in a grateful frame of mind?*

Meditation for the Day

God can work through me better when I am not hurrying. I go very slowly, very quietly, from one duty to the next, taking time to rest and pray between. I make sure I am not too busy. I take everything in order. I venture often into the rest of God and find peace.

Prayer for the Day

I pray that I may take time out often
to rest with God.

AA Thought for the Day

We alcoholics used so little self-control when we were drinking, we were so absolutely selfish, that it does us good to give up something once in awhile. Using self-discipline and denying ourselves a few things is good for us. *Am I practicing enough self-discipline?*

Meditation for the Day

I must try to be guided by God in all human relationships. I cannot accomplish much of value in dealing with people until God knows I am ready. I alone do not have the power or wisdom to put things right between people. I must rely on God to help me in these vital matters.

Prayer for the Day

I pray that I may rely on God in dealing with people's problems. I pray that I may try to follow his guidance in all personal relationships.

AA Thought for the Day

One thing that keeps us sober is a feeling of loyalty to the other members of the group. We know we'd be letting them down if we ever took a drink. When we were drinking, we weren't loyal to anyone. *Am I loyal to my group?*

Meditation for the Day

Calmness is constructive of good. Agitation is destructive of good. I should not rush into action. I should first "be still and know that he is God." Then I should act only as God directs me through my conscience. Only trust, perfect trust in God, can keep me calm when all around me are agitated.

Prayer for the Day

I pray that I may be calm, so that God can work through me.

AA Thought for the Day

 We can depend on those members of any group who have gone all out for the program. They come to meetings. They work with other alcoholics. We try to be loyal members of the group. If we're tempted to take a drink, we tell ourselves that if we did we'd be letting down the other members, who are the best friends we have. *Am I going to let them down, if I can help it?*

Meditation for the Day

Wherever there is true fellowship and love between people, God's spirit is always there as the Divine Third. When a life is changed through the channel of another person, it is God, the Divine Third, who always makes the change, using the person as a means. No personal relationships can be entirely right without the presence of God's spirit.

Prayer for the Day

I pray that I may feel that the Divine Third is always there to help me.

AA Thought for the Day

When we come into AA, looking for a way out of drinking, we really need a lot more than that. We need fellowship. We need to get the things that are troubling us out into the open. We need a new outlet for our energies, and we need a new strength beyond ourselves that will help us face life instead of running away from it. In AA we find these things that we need. *Have I found the things that I need?*

Meditation for the Day

I turn out all thoughts of doubt and fear and resentment. I do not tolerate them if I can help it. I bar the windows and doors of my mind against them, as I would bar my home against a thief who wants to steal my treasures. What greater treasures can I have than faith and courage and love?

Prayer for the Day

*I pray that I may have protection and safety
even in the midst of the storms of life.*

AA Thought for the Day

 In AA we find fellowship and release and strength. And having found these things, the real reasons for our drinking are taken away. Then drinking has no more justification in our minds. At first, we are sorry that we can't drink, but we get so that we are glad that we don't have to drink. *Am I glad that I don't have to drink?*

Meditation for the Day

I try never to judge. Each mind is so different, directed by such different motives, controlled by such different circumstances, influenced by such different sufferings; I cannot know all the influences that have gone to make up a personality. But God knows that person wholly.

Prayer for the Day

I pray that I will not judge other people.

AA Thought for the Day

Having gotten over drinking, we have only just begun to enjoy the benefits of AA. We find new friends, so that we are no longer lonely. We find new relationships with our families, so that we are happy at home. We find release from our troubles and worries through a new way of looking at things. We find an outlet for our energies in helping other people. *Am I enjoying these benefits of AA?*

Meditation for the Day

The kingdom of heaven is within me. God sees, as no one can see, what is within me. He sees me growing more and more like himself. That is my reason for existence, to grow more and more like God, to develop more and more the spirit of God within me.

Prayer for the Day

I pray that I may not expect complete understanding from others. I pray that I may only expect this from God, as I try to grow more like him.

AA Thought for the Day

In AA we find a new strength and peace from the realization that there must be a Power greater than ourselves that is running the universe and that is on our side when we live a good life. So the AA program really never ends. *Am I really enjoying the full benefits of AA?*

Meditation for the Day

"Seek first the kingdom of God and his righteousness, and all these things shall be yours as well." I should not seek material things first, but seek spiritual things first and material things will come to me, as I honestly work for them. The first requirements for an abundant life are the spiritual things: honesty, purity, unselfishness, and love. Until I have these qualities, quantities of material things are of little real use to me.

Prayer for the Day

I pray that I will not expect good things until I am right spiritually.

AA Thought for the Day

 In the story of the good Samaritan, the wayfarer fell among robbers and was left lying in the gutter, half dead. A priest and a Levite both passed by on the other side of the road. But the good Samaritan was moved with compassion and came to him and bound up his wounds and brought him to an inn and took care of him. *Do I treat another alcoholic the way the priest and the Levite did or the way the good Samaritan did?*

Meditation for the Day

Prayer changes things. I practice praying until my trust in God becomes strong. And then I pray on, because it has become so much a habit that I need it daily. I pray until prayer becomes communion with God.

Prayer for the Day

I pray that I may form the habit of daily prayer.

AA Thought for the Day

Alcoholics have fallen for alcohol, in the same way as the man in the Good Samaritan story fell among robbers. The member of AA who is working with others is like the good Samaritan. Are we moved with compassion? *Do I take care of another alcoholic whenever I can?*

Meditation for the Day

I must constantly live in preparation for something better to come. All of life is a preparation for something better. I know that God has something better in store for me, as long as I am making myself ready for it. All my existence in this world is a training for a better life to come.

Prayer for the Day

I pray that when life is over, I will return to an eternal, spaceless life with God. I pray that I may make this life a preparation for a better life to come.

AA Thought for the Day

 We're in AA for two main reasons: to keep sober ourselves and to help others to keep sober. It's a well-known fact that helping others is a big part of keeping sober ourselves. *Do I know that I can't stay sober successfully alone?*

Meditation for the Day

I look by faith into that place beyond space or time where God dwells and from which I came and to which I will eventually return. To look beyond material things is within the power of everyone's imagination. Faith's look saves me from despair. Faith's look saves me from worry and care.

Prayer for the Day

I pray that by faith I may look beyond the now to eternal life.

AA Thought for the Day

Sometimes we don't feel like going to a meeting and we think of excuses for not going. But we usually end up going anyway. And we always get some lift out of every meeting. Meetings are part of keeping sober. And we get more out of a meeting if we try to contribute something to it. *Am I contributing my share at meetings?*

Meditation for the Day

By turning to God and putting my problems in his hands, I am able to overcome my sins and temptations. When I trust God in all things, I have true security. If I honestly try to live the way God wants me to live, I will have God's guidance in my daily living.

Prayer for the Day

I pray that I may rely on God
to guide my comings and goings.

AA Thought for the Day

Witnessing and confession are part of keeping sober. We never know when we may help someone. Helping others is one of the best ways to stay sober. And the satisfaction we get out of helping a fellow human being is one of the finest experiences we can have. *Am I helping others?*

Meditation for the Day

Without God, no real victory is ever won. All the military victories of great conquerors have passed into history. The real victories are won in the spiritual realm. "One who conquers oneself is greater than one who conquers a city."

Prayer for the Day

I pray that with God I will win
the real victory over myself.

AA Thought for the Day

The more we share the more we have. In our old drinking days, we didn't do much sharing. We used to keep things to ourselves, partly because we were ashamed, but mostly because we were selfish. And we were very lonely because we didn't share. *Am I sharing?*

Meditation for the Day

Character is developed by the daily discipline of duties done. I need a life of prayer and meditation, but I must still do my work in the busy ways of life.

Prayer for the Day

I pray that if I fall,
I will pick myself up and go on.

AA Thought for the Day

What impresses us most at an AA meeting is the willingness to share, without holding anything back. Pretty soon we find ourselves sharing, also. And the more we share, the more we have left for ourselves. *Do I know that the more I share, the better chance I'll have to stay sober?*

Meditation for the Day

I should constantly claim God's strength. Once convinced of the right of a course of action, once reasonably sure of God's guidance, I can claim all the strength I need to meet any situation. I have a right to claim it, and I should use my right.

Prayer for the Day

I pray that I may claim God's strength whenever I need it.

AA Thought for the Day

 The Twelfth Step of AA, working with others, can be subdivided into five parts, five words beginning with the letter C—confidence, confession, conviction, conversion, and continuance. The first thing in trying to help other alcoholics is to get their confidence. We do this by telling them our own experiences with drinking, so that they see that we know what we're talking about. *Do I care enough about other alcoholics to get their confidence?*

Meditation for the Day

I must prepare for the future by doing the right thing at the right time now. I should look upon myself as performing God's errands and then coming back to him to tell him in quiet communion that the message has been delivered or the task done.

Prayer for the Day

*I pray that I may leave the outcome
of my actions to God.*

AA Thought for the Day

 In Twelfth Step work, the second thing is confession. By frankly sharing with prospects, we get them talking about their own experiences. They will open up and confess things to us that they haven't been able to tell other people. They feel a sense of release and freedom when they have opened up their hearts to us. *Do I care enough about other alcoholics to help them to make a confession?*

Meditation of the Day

Every troubled soul that God puts in my path is the one for me to help. As I sincerely try to help, a supply of strength will flow into me from God. My circle of helpfulness will widen more and more. I must never say that I have only enough strength for my own need. The more I give away, the more I will keep. That which I keep to myself, I will lose in the end.

Prayer for the Day

I pray that I may have a sincere willingness to give.

AA Thought for the Day

In Twelfth Step work, the third thing is conviction. Prospects must be convinced that they honestly want to stop drinking. They must see and admit that their lives are unmanageable. They must be convinced that they must give up drinking, and they must see that their whole lives depend on this conviction. *Do I care enough about other alcoholics to help them reach this conviction?*

Meditation for the Day

There is no limit to what I can accomplish in helping others. I keep that thought always. I do not give up the thought of any accomplishment because it seems beyond my power. God will help me in all good work. I only give it up if I feel that it's not God's will for me.

Prayer for the Day

I pray that I may always rely
on the power of God to help me.

AA Thought for the Day

In Twelfth Step work, the fourth thing is conversion. Prospects must learn to change their way of thinking. Until now, everything they've done has been connected with drinking. Now they must face a new kind of life, without liquor. They must see and admit that they cannot overcome drinking by their own willpower, so they must turn to a Higher Power for help. *Do I care enough about other alcoholics to help them to make this conversion?*

Meditation for the Day

Discipline is absolutely necessary before the power of God is given to me. When I see others manifesting the power of God, I probably have not seen the discipline that went before. They made themselves ready. All my life is a preparation for more good to be accomplished when God knows that I am ready for it.

Prayer for the Day

I pray that I may discipline myself in order to be ready to meet every opportunity.

AA Thought for the Day

In Twelfth Step work, the fifth thing is continuance. Continuance means staying with prospects after they have started on the new way of living. We must stick with them and not let them down. Continuance means good sponsorship. *Do I care enough about other alcoholics to continue with them as long as necessary?*

Meditation for the Day

Every strong and beautiful flower must have a strong root in the ground. It must send a root down so that it may be grounded while at the same time it sends a shoot up to be the flower that gladdens the world. Both growths are necessary. The higher the growth upward, the deeper must be the rooting.

Prayer for the Day

I pray that my life may be deeply rooted in faith.

AA Thought for the Day

In AA we learn that since we are alcoholics we can be uniquely useful people. The AAs are a unique group of people because we have taken our own greatest defeat and failure and sickness and used it as a means of helping others. We who have been through this are the ones who can best help other alcoholics. *Do I believe that I can be uniquely useful?*

Meditation for the Day

I should try to practice the presence of God. I can feel that he is with me and near me, protecting and strengthening me always. Just to believe that he is near me brings strength and peace. I should try to live as though God were beside me.

Prayer for the Day

*I pray that I may try to practice the presence of God.
I pray that by doing so I may never feel alone
or helpless again.*

AA Thought for the Day

We who have learned to put our drinking problem in God's hands can help others to do so. We can be used as a connection between an alcoholic's need and God's supply of strength. We in Alcoholics Anonymous can be uniquely useful, just because we have the misfortune or fortune to be alcoholics ourselves. *Will I use my own greatest defeat and failure and sickness as a weapon to help others?*

Meditation for the Day

I will try to help others. I will try not to let a day pass without reaching out an arm of love to someone. In my own gratitude, I will turn and help other alcoholics with the burden that is pressing too heavily upon them.

Prayer for the Day

I pray that I may be used by God
to lighten many burdens.

AA Thought for the Day

 AA may be human in its organization, but it is divine in its purpose. The purpose is to point us toward God and a better life. Participating in the privilege of the movement, we will share in the responsibilities, taking it upon ourselves to carry our fair share of the load, joyfully. To the extent that we succeed, AA succeeds. *Do I accept this as my AA credo?*

Meditation for the Day

"Praise the Lord." What does praising God mean? It means being grateful for all the wonderful things in the universe and for all the blessings in my life. So I praise God by being grateful and humble. The truly grateful and humble person, who is always praising God, is not tempted to do wrong.

Prayer for the Day

I pray that I may be grateful for all my blessings.

AA Thought for the Day

 We will not wait to be drafted for service to AA. We will volunteer. We will be loyal in our attendance, generous in our giving, kind in our criticism, creative in our suggestions, loving in our attitudes. We will give to AA our interest, our enthusiasm, our devotion, and most of all, ourselves. *Do I also accept this as my AA credo?*

Meditation for the Day

Prayer is of many kinds, but of whatever kind, prayer is the linking up of the soul and mind to God. The soul, being linked and united to God, receives from him all spiritual help needed. The soul, when in its human body, still needs the things belonging to its heavenly habitation.

Prayer for the Day

I pray that I may be linked through prayer
to the mind and will of God.

JUNE

AA Thought for the Day

 Some things we do not miss since becoming dry: that overall awful feeling physically, including the shakes, a splitting headache, pains in our arms and legs, bleary eyes, fluttering stomachs, droopy shoulders, weak knees, and a flushed complexion. *I don't miss these things, do I?*

Meditation for the Day

I was born with a spark of the Divine within me. It had been all but smothered by the life I was living. That celestial fire has to be tended and fed so that it will grow eventually into a real desire to live the right way. By trying to do the will of God, I grow more and more in the new way of life. By thinking of God, praying to him, and having communion with him, I gradually grow more like him.

Prayer for the Day

I pray that I may tend the spark of the Divine within me so that it will grow.

AA Thought for the Day

Some more things we do not miss since becoming dry: wondering if the car is in the garage and how we got home, struggling to remember where we were and what we did since our last conscious moment, dreading the day ahead of us. *I'm quite sure that I don't miss these things, am I not?*

Meditation for the Day

The gradual elimination of selfishness in the growth of love for God and my fellow human beings is the goal of life. At first, I have only a faint likeness to the Divine, but the picture grows and takes on more and more of the likeness of God until those who see me can see in me some of the power of God's grace at work in a human life.

Prayer for the Day

I pray that I may develop that faint likeness
I have to the Divine.

AA Thought for the Day

Some more things we do not miss since becoming dry: meeting friends and trying to cover up that we feel awful, looking at ourselves in a mirror and calling ourselves fools, struggling with ourselves to snap out of it for two or three days, wondering what it is all about. *I'm positive I don't miss these things, am I not?*

Meditation for the Day

Love is the power that transforms my life. I try to love my family and friends and then try to love everybody that I possibly can—everybody. Love for God is an even greater thing. It is the result of gratitude to God. I say, "Thank you, God," until it becomes a habit.

Prayer for the Day

I pray that I may try to love God and all people.

AA Thought for the Day

Some things we like since becoming dry: feeling good in the morning, full use of our intelligence, joy in our activities, the love and trust of family, lack of remorse, the confidence of friends, the prospect of a happy future, the appreciation of the beauties of nature, knowing what it is all about. *I'm sure that I like these things, am I not?*

Meditation for the Day

Molding my life means cutting and shaping my material into something good, something that can express the spiritual. All material things are the clay out of which we mold something spiritual. As the work of molding proceeds, I see more and more clearly what must be done to mold my life into something better.

Prayer for the Day

*I pray that I may mold my life
into something useful and good. I pray that
I will not be discouraged by slow progress.*

AA Thought for the Day

 We alcoholics are fortunate to be living in a day and age when there is such a thing as Alcoholics Anonymous. Before AA came into being, there was very little hope for the alcoholic. AA is a great rebuilder of human wreckage. *Have I found a better way of living?*

Meditation for the Day

Very quietly God speaks through my thoughts and feelings. I heed the divine voice of my conscience. If I listen for this I will never be disappointed in the results in my life. I listen for this small, still voice and my tired nerves become rested. The divine voice comes to me as strength as well as tenderness, as power as well as restfulness.

Prayer for the Day

I pray that I may listen for the still, small voice of God. I pray that I may obey the leading of my conscience.

AA Thought for the Day

 Drinking is the way we alcoholics express our maladjustments to life. Many of us had an inferiority complex. We didn't make friends easily. There was a wall between us and other people. And we were lonely. We were not well adjusted to life. *Did I drink to escape from myself?*

Meditation for the Day

The weak need God's strength. The strong need God's tenderness. The tempted and fallen need God's saving grace. The righteous need God's pity for sinners. The lonely need God as a friend. The fighters for righteousness need a leader in God. I may think of God in any way I wish.

Prayer for the Day

I pray that I may think of God
as supplying my needs.

AA Thought for the Day

 Alcoholism is a progressive illness. We go through the three stages of social drinking, trouble drinking, and merry-go-round drinking. We land in hospitals and jails. We eventually lose our friends, our families, and our self-respect. Yes, alcoholism is a progressive illness and there are only three ends to it—the insane asylum, the morgue, or total abstinence. *Will I choose not to take the first drink?*

Meditation for the Day

I not only can live a new life but I can also grow in grace and power and beauty. I reach ever forward and upward after the things of the spirit. My whole character changes as I reach upward for the things of the spirit—for beauty, for love, for honesty, for purity, and for unselfishness.

Prayer for the Day

I pray that I may reach forward and upward.

AA Thought for the Day

 Once an alcoholic, always an alcoholic. We are never cured. Our alcoholism can only be paused. No matter how long we have been sober, if we try liquor again, we're as bad as or worse than we ever were. There is no exception to this rule in the whole history of AA. *Will I try to recapture the good times of the past?*

Meditation for the Day

My life has been given to me mainly for the purpose of training my soul. We often choose the way of life that best suits the body, not the way that best suits the soul. God wants me to choose what suits the soul as well as the body. My soul is being trained by the good I choose. Thus the purpose of my life is being accomplished.

Prayer for the Day

I pray that I may choose what is good for my soul.

AA Thought for the Day

We finally came to the bottom. We did not have to be financially broke, although many of us were. But we were spiritually bankrupt. We had a soul-sickness, a revulsion against ourselves and against our way of living. Life had become impossible for us. We had to end it all or do something about it. *Am I glad I did something about it?*

Meditation for the Day

I must try to make a union between my purposes and the purposes of God. By trying to merge my mind with the mind of God, a oneness of purpose results. This oneness of purpose puts me in harmony with God and others. Good comes from being in harmony with him.

Prayer for the Day

I pray that I may get into the stream of goodness in the universe.

AA Thought for the Day

 If we have had some moral, religious, or spiritual training, we're better prospects for AA. When we reach the bottom, at this crucial moment when we're thoroughly licked, we turn instinctively to whatever decency is left in us. We call upon whatever reserves of morality and faith are left down deep in our heart. *Have I had this spiritual experience?*

Meditation for the Day

The world sees the person of faith make a demand on God's stores of power and the demand is met. The world does not see what that person has been putting in, in thanks and praise, in prayer and communion, in small good deeds done faithfully, steadily over the years.

Prayer for the Day

I pray that I may keep making deposits
in God's bank. I pray that in my hour of need,
I may call upon these.

AA Thought for the Day

 We alcoholics have to believe in some Power greater than ourselves. Yes, we have to believe in God. *Have I stopped trying to run my own life?*

Meditation for the Day

To know peace is to have received the stamp of the kingdom of God. When I have earned that peace, I am fit to judge between true and false values, between the values of the kingdom of God and the values of all that the world has to offer.

Prayer for the Day

*I pray that today I may be
at peace with myself.*

AA Thought for the Day

When we came into AA, we made a tremendous discovery. We found that we were sick persons rather than moral lepers. We found other people who had been through the same experiences that we had been through. They had recovered. If they could do it, we could do it. *Was hope born in me the day I walked into AA?*

Meditation for the Day

"Every one then who hears these words of mine and does them will be like a wise man who built his house upon the rock; and the rain fell, and the floods came, and the winds blew and beat upon that house, but it did not fall, because it had been founded on the rock." When my life is built upon obedience to God and upon doing his will as I understand it, I will be steadfast and unmovable even in the midst of storms.

Prayer for the Day

I pray that I may be obedient to the heavenly vision.

AA Thought for the Day

 In AA we have to reeducate our minds. We have to learn to think differently. We have to take a long view of drinking instead of a short view. We have to look through the glass to what lies beyond it. We have to look through the night before to the morning after. *Have I learned to look through the bottle to the better life that lies ahead?*

Meditation for the Day

If I am honestly trying to live the way I believe God wants me to live, I can get guidance from God in times of quiet communion with him, provided my thoughts are directed toward God's will and all good things. The attitude of "Thy will, not mine, be done" leads to clear guidance. If I act on this guidance, I will be led to better things.

Prayer for the Day

*I pray that my thoughts may be guided
by his thoughts.*

AA Thought for the Day

In AA we have to learn that drink is our greatest enemy. Although we used to think that liquor was our friend, the time came when it turned against us and became our enemy. We realize now that liquor is our enemy. *Is it still my main business to keep sober?*

Meditation for the Day

It is not my circumstances that need altering so much as myself. After I have changed, conditions will naturally change. I spare no effort to become all that God wants me to become. I follow every good leading of my conscience. I seek God's help and guidance as to what I should do in every situation that may arise. I never look back. I never leave until tomorrow the thing that I am guided to do today.

Prayer for the Day

I pray that God will help me to become all that he would have me be.

AA Thought for the Day

 In AA we have three things: fellowship, faith, and service. Fellowship is wonderful, but its wonder lasts just so long. Then some gossip, disillusionment, and boredom may come in. Worry and fear come back at times, and we find that fellowship is not the whole story. Then we need faith. When we're alone, with nobody to pat us on the back, we must turn to God for help. *Can I say, "Thy will be done"—and mean it?*

Meditation for the Day

There is beauty in a God-guided life. There is wonder in the feeling of being led by God. God is planning for me. Wonderful are his ways— they are beyond my knowledge. God's leading will enter my consciousness more and more and bring me ever more peace and joy.

Prayer for the Day

I pray that I may develop the feeling of being led by God.

AA Thought for the Day

But even faith is not the whole story. There must be service. We must give this thing away if we want to keep it. To be of service to other people makes our lives worth living. *Does service to others give me a real purpose in life?*

Meditation for the Day

I seek God early in the day, before he gets crowded out by life's problems, difficulties, or pleasures. In that early quiet time I gain a calm, strong confidence in the goodness and purpose in the universe. I do not seek God only when the world's struggles prove too much and too many for me to bear or face alone.

Prayer for the Day

I pray that I may seek God early and often.

AA Thought for the Day

 We in AA have the privilege of living two lives in one lifetime. One life of drunkenness, failure, and defeat. Then, through AA, another life of sobriety, peace of mind, and usefulness. We who have recovered our sobriety are modern miracles. *Do I owe a debt of gratitude to AA that I can never repay as long as I live?*

Meditation for the Day

I think of God as often as possible and use the thought prayerfully and purposefully. It will carry my thoughts away from material things and toward the spiritual things that make life worthwhile.

Prayer for the Day

I pray that I may think of God often. I pray that I may rest in peace at the thought of his love and care.

AA Thought for the Day

The AA way of living is not an easy one. But it's an adventure in living that is really worthwhile. And it's so much better than our old drunken way of living that there's no comparison. Our lives without AA would be worth nothing. It's worth the battle, no matter how tough the going is from day to day. *Isn't it worth the battle?*

Meditation for the Day

A life of prayer and quiet communion with God means that every day my mind can be set in the right direction so that my thoughts will be of the right kind. The victories I have won over myself through the help of God can be shared with others.

Prayer for the Day

*I pray that I may grow strong
from my times apart with God.*

AA Thought for the Day

We have this choice every day of our lives. We can take the path that leads to insanity and death. And remember, our next drunk could be our last one. Or we can take the path that leads to a reasonably happy and useful life. The choice is ours each day of our lives. God grant that we take the right path. *Have I made my choice today?*

Meditation for the Day

My real work in life is to grow spiritually. To do this I must follow the path of diligently seeking good. The hidden spiritual wonders are revealed to those who diligently seek this treasure. From one point to the next, I have to follow the way of obedience to God's will until finally I reach greater and greater spiritual heights.

Prayer for the Day

I pray that I may make spiritual growth my real life's work.

AA Thought for the Day

We strive to live for some purpose greater than ourselves. We have received so much from the AA program that we should have a vision that gives our lives direction and purpose that gives meaning to each new day. Let's not slide along through life. Let's have a purpose for each day, and let's make that purpose for something greater than just ourselves. *What is my purpose for today?*

Meditation for the Day

To see God with eyes of faith is to cause God's power to manifest itself in the material world. God cannot do his work where there is unbelief. In response to my belief, God can work a miracle in my personality. All miracles happen in the realm of personality and all are caused by and based on belief in God's never-failing power.

Prayer for the Day

I pray that I may see God with the eyes of faith.

AA Thought for the Day

 Intelligent faith in that Power greater than ourselves can be counted on to stabilize our emotions. We look up, around, and away from ourselves, and we see that nine out of ten things that at the moment upset us will shortly disappear. Problems solve themselves, criticism and unkindness vanish as though they had never been. *Do I have the proper perspective toward life?*

Meditation for the Day

The only way to keep calm in this troubled world is to have a serene mind. The calm and sane mind sees spiritual things as the true realities and material things as only temporary and fleeting.

Prayer for the Day

I pray that I may have a calm and sane mind.

AA Thought for the Day

When we allow ourselves to be upset over one thing, we succeed only in opening the door to the coming of hundreds of other upsetting things. *Am I allowing myself to be upset over little things?*

Meditation for the Day

I would do well not to think of the Red Sea of difficulties that lies ahead. I am sure that when I come to that Red Sea, the waters will part and I will be given all the power I need to face and overcome many difficulties and meet what is in store for me with courage.

Prayer for the Day

I pray that I may face the future with courage.

AA Thought for the Day

 No chain is stronger than its weakest link. Likewise, if we fail in the day-by-day program, in all probability it will be at our weakest point. Great faith and constant contact with God's power can help us discover, guard, and undergird our weakest point with a strength not our own. Intelligent faith in God's power can be counted on to help us master our emotions. *Am I master of my emotions?*

Meditation for the Day

I need to be constantly recharged by the power of the spirit of God. I commune with God in quiet times until the life from God, the divine life, by that very contact, flows into my being and revives my fainting spirit. When weary, I take time out and rest. I rest until every care and worry and fear have gone.

Prayer for the Day

I pray that I may pause and wait
for the renewing of my strength.

AA Thought for the Day

Alcohol is our weakness. We suffer from mental conflicts that we try to escape by drowning our problems in drink. We try through drink to push away from the realities of life. But alcohol does not feed, alcohol does not build; it only borrows from the future and it ultimately destroys. *Do I have control over my unstable emotions?*

Meditation for the Day

When I let personal resentments interfere with what I know to be my proper conduct, I am on the wrong track and I am undoing all I have built up by doing the right thing. I must not weaken my spiritual power by letting personal resentments upset me.

Prayer for the Day

I pray that I may go quietly along the path I have chosen.

AA Thought for the Day

One of the most encouraging facts of life is that our weaknesses can become our greatest assets. Our weaknesses can become assets if we will face them, examine them, and trace them to their origins. Set each weakness in the very center of our minds. No weakness, such as drinking, ever turned into an asset until it was first fairly faced. *Am I making my weakness my greatest asset?*

Meditation for the Day

Whenever I seek to worship God, I can think of the great universe that God rules over, of creation, of mighty law and order throughout the universe. Then I will feel the awe that precedes worship.

Prayer for the Day

I pray that I may accept the limitless and eternal Spirit. I pray that it may express itself in my life.

AA Thought for the Day

We must know the nature of our weakness before we can determine how to deal with it. When we are honest about its presence, we may discover that it is imaginary and can be overcome by a change of thinking. *Have I fully accepted my handicap?*

Meditation for the Day

There is a proper time for everything. I must learn not to do things at the wrong time, that is, before I am ready or before conditions are right. Timing is important. I must learn, in the little daily situations of life, to delay action until I am sure that I am doing the right thing at the right time.

Prayer for the Day

I pray that I will not rush in alone.

AA Thought for the Day

 If we can take our troubles as they come, if we can maintain calm and composure amid pressing duties and unending engagements, if we can rise above the distressing and disturbing circumstances in which we are set down, we have discovered a priceless secret of daily living. *Have I achieved poise and peace of mind?*

Meditation for the Day

I take a blessing with me wherever I go. I have been blessed, so I bless others. If I shed a little blessing in the heart of one person, that person is cheered to pass it on, and so God's vitalizing, joy-giving message travels on.

Prayer for the Day

I pray that I may pass on my blessings.

JUNE 28

AA Thought for the Day

Just try to remember what troubled us most a week ago. We probably will find it difficult to remember. Why then should we unduly worry or fret over the problems that arise today? Our attitudes toward them can be changed by putting ourselves and our problems in God's hands and trusting him to see that everything will turn out all right, provided we are trying to do the right thing. *Has my mental attitude changed?*

Meditation for the Day

I cannot see the future. It's a blessing that I cannot. I could not bear to know all the future. That is why God only reveals it to me day by day. God is powerful enough to do anything he wills, and no miracle in human lives is impossible with him.

Prayer for the Day

*I pray that I may gladly leave my future
in God's hands.*

AA Thought for the Day

The program of Alcoholics Anonymous involves a continuous striving for improvement. There can be no long resting period. We must try to work at it all the time. It is a timeless program in every sense. We live it day by day, or more precisely, moment by moment—now. *Am I always striving for improvement?*

Meditation for the Day

Life is all a preparation for something better to come. God has a plan for my life and it will work out, if I try to do his will. God has things planned for me, far beyond what I can imagine now. Now is the time for discipline and prayer. The time of expression will come later.

Prayer for the Day

I pray that I may prepare myself for better things that God has in store for me.

AA Thought for the Day

 Alcoholics are unable or unwilling, during their addiction to alcohol, to live in the present. The result is that they live in a constant state of remorse and fear. So the only real hope for the alcoholic is to face the present. Now is the time. Now is ours. *Am I living in the now?*

Meditation for the Day

I must forget the past as much as possible. The past is over and gone forever. Nothing can be done about the past, except to make what restitution I can. I must not carry the burden of my past failures. I must go on in faith.

Prayer for the Day

I pray that I will not carry the burden of the past.

JULY

AA Thought for the Day

 Day after day our sobriety results in the formation of new habits, normal habits. As each twenty-four-hour period ends, we find that the business of staying sober is a much less trying and fearsome ordeal than it seemed in the beginning. *Do I find it easier as I go along?*

Meditation for the Day

For all kinds of people, this should be the attitude: a loving desire to help and an infectious spirit of calmness and trust in God. I have the answer to loneliness and fear, which is calm faith in the goodness and purpose in the universe.

Prayer for the Day

I pray that I may be calm in the midst of storms.

AA Thought for the Day

 We have the advantage of sincere friendship and understanding of the other AA members who, through social and personal contact, take us away from our old haunts and environments. We find in this association a sympathy and a willingness on the part of most members to do everything in their power to help us. *Do I appreciate the wonderful fellowship of AA?*

Meditation for the Day

"Unless you become like children, you will never enter the kingdom of heaven." All who seek heaven on earth or in the hereafter should become like little children. Even as I grow older, the years of seeking can give me the attitude of the trusting child. Not only for its simple trust should I have the childlike spirit, but also for its joy in life, its ready laughter, its lack of criticism, and its desire to share.

Prayer for the Day

I pray that I may become like a child
in faith and hope.

AA Thought for the Day

 In the beginning of Alcoholics Anonymous there were only two persons. Now there are many groups and thousands of members. Our Higher Power works for good in all things and helps us to accomplish much in individual growth and in the growth of AA groups. *Am I doing my part in helping AA to grow?*

Meditation for the Day

"Blessed are they that hunger and thirst after righteousness, for they shall be filled." Much of life is spiritually unexplored country. Only to the consecrated and loving people who walk with God in spirit can these great spiritual discoveries be revealed. I keep going forward and keep growing in righteousness.

Prayer for the Day

I pray that I may let God lead me forward.

AA Thought for the Day

In Alcoholics Anonymous there is no thought of individual profit. No greed or gain. No membership fees, no dues. All that we hope for is sobriety and regeneration, so that we can live normal, respectable lives. These things we accomplish by the help of each other, by following the Twelve Steps, and by the grace of God. *Am I willing to work for AA without material gain to myself?*

Meditation for the Day

What is sometimes called a conversion by religion is often only the discovery of God as a friend in need. What is sometimes called religion is often only the experiencing of the help and strength of God's power. What is sometimes called holiness is often only the invitation of God to be a Friend.

Prayer for the Day

I pray that I may think of God as a Great Friend in need. I pray that I may go along with him.

AA Thought for the Day

 Until we came into AA most of us had tried desperately to stop drinking. We were filled with the delusion that we could drink like our friends. We tried time and again to take it or leave it, but we could do neither. We wanted to stop. We realized that every reason for drinking was only a crazy excuse. *Have I given up every excuse for drinking?*

Meditation for the Day

I cannot forever stand against God's will for me, nor can I forever upset God's plan for my life, even though God's plan may be postponed by my willfullness and deliberate choice. A whole world of men and women cannot permanently change God's laws or his purpose for the universe.

Prayer for the Day

I pray that I may accept God's direction in my life's journey.

AA Thought for the Day

We tried to study our alcoholic problem, wondering what was the cause of our strange obsession. We tried through crazy excuses to convince ourselves that we knew why we drank, but we went on regardless. We had become alcoholics, destroying ourselves against our own will. *Am I completely free from my alcoholic obsession?*

Meditation for the Day

"Ask and you will receive." I can do practically anything in the field of human relationships, if I am willing to call on God's supply of strength. The supply may not be immediately available, because I may not be entirely ready to receive it. But it will surely come when I am properly prepared for it.

Prayer for the Day

I pray that I may claim God's supply of strength by my faith in him.

AA Thought for the Day

Many drinkers have said, "I hadn't gone that far; I still had my family; I managed to keep out of jail. True, I took too much sometimes and I guess I managed to make quite a fool of myself when I did, but I still thought I could control my drinking. I didn't really believe that I was an alcoholic." *If I was one of these, have I fully changed my mind?*

Meditation for the Day

Painful as the present time may be, I will one day see the reason for it. I will see that it was not only testing, but also a preparation for the life-work that I am to do.

Prayer for the Day

I pray that I may be willing to go through a time of testing. I pray that I may trust God for the outcome.

AA Thought for the Day

 AA members say they can look back and clearly see that they were out of control long before they finally admitted it. Every one of us has gone through that stage when we wouldn't admit that we were alcoholics. *Have I any reservations as to my status as an alcoholic?*

Meditation for the Day

There is a force for good in the world, and when I am cooperating with that force for good, good things happen to me. This force for good is God's will. God wants me to bring all of my desires into oneness with his desires. He works through people. If I try to make God's will my will, I will be in the stream of goodness, carried along by everything that is right.

Prayer for the Day

I pray that I may try to make God's will my will.

AA Thought for the Day

Many people are creeping through life on their hands and knees, merely because they refuse to rely on any power but themselves. Many of them feel that they are being brave and independent, but actually they are only courting disaster. Anxiety and the inferiority complex have become the greatest of all modern plagues. In AA we have the answer to these ills. *Have I ceased to rely on myself only?*

Meditation for the Day

When I am in doubt, I am not going anywhere. Doubt poisons all action. I meet life with a "yes," an affirmative attitude. There is good in the world, and I can follow that good. There is power available to help me to do the right thing; therefore I will accept that power.

Prayer for the Day

I pray that I may go along on the venture of faith.

AA Thought for the Day

 We in Alcoholics Anonymous do not enter into theological discussions, but in carrying our message we attempt to explain the simple "how" of the spiritual life. How faith in a Higher Power can help us to overcome loneliness, fear, and anxiety. How it can help us get along with other people. How it can make it possible for us to rise above pain, sorrow, and despondency. How it can help us to overcome our desires for the things that destroy. *Have I reached a simple, effective faith?*

Meditation for the Day

Expect miracles of change in people's lives. Do not be held back by unbelief. People can be changed, and they are often ready and waiting to be changed. Modern miracles happen every day in the lives of people.

Prayer for the Day

I pray that I may have the faith to expect miracles.

JULY 11

AA Thought for the Day

We in Alcoholics Anonymous tell the newcomer that we have renewed our faith in a Higher Power. In the telling, our faith is further renewed. We believe there is a force for good in the universe and that if we link up with this force, we are carried onward to a new life. *Am I in this stream of goodness?*

Meditation for the Day

I can face all things through the power of God, which strengthens me. Once God has set on me his stamp and seal of ownership, all his strength will serve and protect me. God will do all that is necessary for my spiritual well-being, if I will let him live his way.

Prayer for the Day

I pray that I may rely on God as I go through this day. I pray that I may feel deeply secure, no matter what happens to me.

AA Thought for the Day

Today is ours. Let us live today as we believe God wants us to live. Each day will have a new pattern that we cannot foresee. But we can open each day with a quiet period in which we say a little prayer, asking God to help us through the day. Personal contact with God, as we understand him, will from day to day bring us nearer to an understanding of his will for us. At the close of the day, we offer him thanks for another day of sobriety. *Am I asking God each day for strength and thanking him each night?*

Meditation for the Day

If I believe that God's grace has saved me, then I must believe that he is meaning to save me even more and to keep me in the way that I should go. God will complete the task he sets out to do.

Prayer for the Day

I pray that I may trust God to keep me in the way.

AA Thought for the Day

 Before alcoholics come into AA, they are "flying blind." But AA gives them a directed beam in the AA program. As long as they keep on this beam, the signal of sobriety keeps coming through. If they have a slip, the signal is broken. If they swing off course into drunkenness, the signal stops. Unless they regain the AA-directed beam, they are in danger of crashing against the mountain peak of despair. *Am I on the beam?*

Meditation for the Day

I must be expectant. I must constantly expect better things. I believe that what God has in store for me is better than anything I ever had before. The way to grow old happily is to expect better things right up to the end of my life and even beyond that.

Prayer for the Day

I pray that I may wait with complete faith for the next good thing in store for me.

AA Thought for the Day

In our drinking days, we had no peace of mind or serenity. We had the exact opposite, a kind of turmoil and that "quiet desperation" we knew so well. The turmoil of our drinking days was caused partly by our physical suffering, the terrible hangovers, the cold sweats, the shakes, and the jitters. But it was caused even more by our mental suffering, the loneliness, the feeling of inferiority, the lying, the remorse that every alcoholic understands. *Have I achieved more peace of mind?*

Meditation for the Day

I try to look for God's leading in all my personal relationships, in all my dealings with other persons. God will help me to take care of all my relationships with people, if I am willing to let him guide me.

Prayer for the Day

I pray that I may go forward today unafraid.

AA Thought for the Day

After we had sobered up through the AA program, we gradually began to get a peace of mind and serenity that we never thought were possible. This peace of mind is based on a feeling that fundamentally all is well. Little things can keep going wrong and big things can keep on upsetting us. But deep down in our hearts we know that everything is eventually going to be all right, now that we are living sober lives. *Have I achieved a deep down, inner calm?*

Meditation for the Day

I am climbing up the ladder of life, which reaches into eternity. Would God plant my feet upon an insecure ladder? Its supports may be out of sight, hidden in secret places, but if God has asked me to step on and up firmly, then surely he has secured my ladder. Faith gives me the strength to climb steadily this ladder of life.

Prayer for the Day

I pray that I may progress steadily through the rest of my life with faith and confidence.

AA Thought for the Day

 It has been said that we should "wear the world like a loose garment." That means that nothing should seriously upset us because we have a deep, abiding faith that God will always take care of us. To us that means not to be too upset by the surface wrongness of things, but to feel deeply secure in the fundamental goodness and purpose in the universe. *Do I feel deeply secure?*

Meditation for the Day

Like the shadow of a great rock in a desert land, God is my refuge from the ills of life. The old hymn says, "Rock of ages cleft for me, let me hide myself in thee." God's power can protect me from every temptation and defeat. I will try to feel his divine power—call on it, accept it, and use it. Armed with that power, I can face anything. Each day, I seek safety in God's secret place, in communion with him.

Prayer for the Day

I pray that I may find a haven
in the thought of God.

AA Thought for the Day

 The new life of sobriety we are learning to live in AA is slowly growing on us, and we are beginning to get some of that deep peace of mind and serenity that we never thought were possible. At first we may have doubted that this could happen to us, but looking at the happy faces around us, we know that somehow it is happening to us. In fact, it cannot help happening to anyone who takes the AA program seriously day by day. *Can I see my own happiness reflected in the faces of others?*

Meditation for the Day

God's presence, his truth, his spirit, his strength are always immediately available to me, whenever I am fully willing to receive them. But they may be blocked off by selfishness, intellectual pride, fear, greed, and materialism. I must try to get rid of these blocks and let God's spirit come in.

Prayer for the Day

I pray that I may remove all blocks
that are keeping me from God.

AA Thought for the Day

 Two things can spoil group unity— gossip and criticism. To avoid these divisive things, we must realize that we're all in the same boat. We're like a group of people in a lifeboat after the steamer has sunk. If we're going to be saved, we've got to pull together. We're all in AA to keep sober ourselves and to help each other to keep sober. And neither gossip nor criticism helps anyone to stay sober. *Am I often guilty of gossip or criticism?*

Meditation for the Day

I should try to be grateful for all the blessings that I have received and do not deserve. Gratitude to God for all his blessings will make me humble. Gratitude to God and true humility are what make me effective.

Prayer for the Day

I pray that I may walk humbly with God. I pray that I may rely on his grace to carry me through.

AA Thought for the Day

 We shouldn't gossip about the relationships of any person in the group. And if we say about another member, "I think she or he is taking a few drinks on the side," it's the worst thing we could do to that person. If someone is not living up to AA principles or has a slip, it's up to her or him to stand up in a meeting and say so. *Do I talk about other members behind their backs?*

Meditation for the Day

There is no miracle in personalities too marvelous to be an everyday happening. But miracles happen only to those who are fully guided and strengthened by God. These miracles have been prepared for by days and months of longing for something better. They are always accompanied by a real desire to conquer self and to surrender one's life to God.

Prayer for the Day

I pray that I may expect miracles
in the lives of people.

JULY 20

AA Thought for the Day

 We must be loyal to the group and to each member of it. We must never accuse members behind their backs or even to their faces. More than that, we must try not to think bad things about any members, because if we do, we're consciously or unconsciously hurting that person. *Am I a loyal member of my group?*

Meditation for the Day

I will carry out God's guidance as best I can and leave the results to him. I do this obediently and faithfully with no question that if the guidance is left in God's hands, the results will be all right. So I follow God's guidance according to my conscience.

Prayer for the Day

I pray that I may live according to the dictates of my conscience. I pray that I may leave the results to God.

AA Thought for the Day

 If we feel the need to put another member on the right track, we should try to be understanding and sympathetic, not critical. We should keep everything out in the open and aboveboard. Gossip and criticism are not tolerance, and tolerance is an AA principle that is absolutely necessary to group unity. *Am I truly tolerant of all of my group's members?*

Meditation for the Day

"Faith can move mountains." If I trust him, God shows me the way to "move mountains." If I am humble enough to know that I can do little by myself to change a situation, if I have enough faith to ask God to give me the power I need, and if I am grateful enough for the grace he gives me, I can "move mountains." Situations will be changed for the better by my presence.

Prayer for the Day

*I pray that I may have enough faith
to make me really effective.*

AA Thought for the Day

One of the finest things about AA is the diversity of its membership. We come from all walks and stations of life. All types and classes of people are represented in an AA group. Being different from each other in certain ways, we can each make a different contribution to the whole. AA can use the strong points of all its members and can disregard their weaknesses. *Do I recognize the good points of all of my group's members?*

Meditation for the Day

"Greater works than these will he do." Each individual has the ability to do good works through the power of God's spirit. This is the wonder of the world, the miracle of the earth, that God's power goes out to bless the human race through the agency of so many people who are moved by his grace.

Prayer for the Day

I pray that I will not limit myself by doubting.

AA Thought for the Day

 We should not set any member upon a pedestal and mark her or him out as a perfect AA. Without exception, we are all only one drink away from a drunk, no matter how long we have been in AA. Nobody is entirely safe. AA itself should be our ideal, not any particular member of it. *Am I putting my trust in AA principles and not in any one member of the group?*

Meditation for the Day

The inward peace that comes from trust in God truly passes all understanding. That peace no one can take from me. But I must be careful to not let in the world's worries and distractions. I must try to not give entrance to fears and despondency. I make it a point to allow nothing today to disturb my inner peace, my heart-calm.

Prayer for the Day

I pray that I may keep a deep inner calm throughout the day.

AA Thought for the Day

AA is like a dike, holding back the ocean of liquor. If we take one glass of liquor, it is like making a small hole in the dike, and once such a hole has been made, the whole ocean of alcohol may rush in upon us. By practicing the AA principles we keep the dike strong and in repair. *Am I keeping the dike strong?*

Meditation for the Day

I keep as close as I can to my Higher Power. I try to think, act, live as though I am always in God's presence. Keeping close to a Power greater than myself is the solution to most of the earth's problems. I try to practice the presence of God in the things I think and do. That is the secret of personal power.

Prayer for the Day

I pray that I may keep close to the mind of God.

AA Thought for the Day

 We are living today because of AA and the grace of God. And what there is left of our lives we owe to AA and to God. We should make the best use we can of our borrowed time and in some small measure pay back for that part of our lives which we wasted before we came into AA. Our lives from now on are not our own. We hold them in trust for God and AA. *Am I holding my life in trust for AA?*

Meditation for the Day

I should hold my life in trust for God. Is anything too much to expect from such a life? Do I begin to see how dedicated a life in trust for God can be? In such a life miracles can happen. If I am faithful, I can believe that God has many good things in store for me. I try to act as God guides and leave all results to him.

Prayer for the Day

I pray that I will no longer consider my life as all my own.

AA Thought for the Day

 When we come to the end of our lives on earth, we will take no material thing with us. We will not take one cent in our cold, dead hands. The only things that we may take are the things we have given away. If we have helped others, we may take that with us. Looking back over our lives, what are we proud of? Not what we have gained for ourselves, but what few good deeds we have done. Those are the things that really matter in the long run. *What will I take with me when I go?*

Meditation for the Day

"Hallowed be thy name." What does that mean to me? Here *name* is used in the sense of *spirit.* The words mean praise to God for his spirit in the world, making me better. His spirit is powerful. It can help me to live a conquering, abundant life.

Prayer for the Day

I pray that I may be grateful for God's spirit in me.

AA Thought for the Day

 The law of AA is perfect, converting the drunk. The testimony of AA is sure, making wise the simple. The statutes of AA are right, rejoicing the heart. The program of AA is pure, enlightening the eyes. The fear of the first drink is clean, enduring forever. *Have I any doubt about the power of liquor?*

Meditation for the Day

"Walk humbly with thy God." Walking with God means practicing the presence of God in my daily affairs. It means asking God for strength to face each new day. It means turning to him often during the day in prayer for myself and for other people. It means thanking him at night for the blessings I have received during the day. Nothing can seriously upset me if I am "walking with God."

Prayer for the Day

I pray that I may try to walk humbly with God.
I pray that I may turn to him often
as to a close friend.

AA Thought for the Day

Cleanse us from secret faults. Keep us from lofty resentments. Let them not have dominance over us. *Am I resolved that liquor will never again have dominance over me?*

Meditation for the Day

God can be my shield. Then no problems of the world can harm me. Between me and all scorn and indignity from others is my trust in God, like a shining shield.

Prayer for the Day

I pray that I may strive for inward peace.

AA Thought for the Day

 There are two days in every week about which we should not worry, two days that should be kept from fear and apprehension. One of these days is yesterday, with its mistakes and cares, its faults and blunders, its aches and pains. Yesterday has passed forever beyond our control. *Do I still worry about what happened yesterday?*

Meditation for the Day

If I have enough faith and trust in God, he will give me all the strength I need to face every temptation and to overcome it. Nothing will prove too difficult for me to bear. I can face any situation. I can overcome any temptation with God's help. So I should not fear anything.

Prayer for the Day

I pray that I may face every situation without fear. I pray that nothing will prove too difficult for me to bear.

AA Thought for the Day

 The other day we should not worry about is tomorrow, with its possible adversities, its burdens, its large promise, and perhaps its poor performance. Tomorrow is also beyond our immediate control. Tomorrow's sun will rise, either in splendor or behind a mask of clouds, but it will rise. Until it does, we have no stake in tomorrow, for it is as yet unborn. *Do I still worry too much about tomorrow?*

Meditation for the Day

Faith is not seeing, but believing. I cannot see God, but I can see the results of faith in human lives, changing them from defeat to victory. God's grace is available to all who have faith— not seeing, but believing. With faith, life can be victorious and happy.

Prayer for the Day

I pray that I may be content
with the results of my faith.

AA Thought for the Day

Anyone can fight the battles of just one day. It is only when you and I add the burden of those two awful eternities, yesterday and tomorrow, that we break down. It is not the experience of today that drives us mad. It is the remorse or bitterness for something that happened yesterday or the dread of what tomorrow may bring. *Am I living one day at a time?*

Meditation for the Day

I give God the gift of a thankful heart. When life seems hard, I look for some reasons for thankfulness. If I seek diligently for something to be glad and thankful about, I will acquire in time the habit of being constantly grateful to God for all his blessings.

Prayer for the Day

I pray that I may be constantly reminded of causes for sincere gratitude.

AUGUST

AA Thought for the Day

 The Alcoholics Anonymous program has borrowed from medicine, psychiatry, and religion. It has taken from these what it wanted and combined them into the program that it considers best suited to the alcoholic mind. We do not try to improve on the AA program. Its value has been proved by the success it has had in helping thousands of alcoholics to recover. *Do I try to follow the AA program just as it is?*

Meditation for the Day

There is no bond of union on earth to compare with the union between a human soul and God. Priceless beyond all earth's rewards is that union. In merging my heart and mind with the heart and mind of my Higher Power, a oneness of purpose results. That oneness of purpose puts me in harmony with God and with all others who are trying to do his will.

Prayer for the Day

*I pray that I may become attuned
to the will of God.*

AA Thought for the Day

 Alcoholics Anonymous has no quarrel with medicine, psychiatry, or religion. We have great respect for the methods of each. And we are glad for any success they may have had with alcoholics. We are desirous always of cooperating with them in every way. *Am I ready to cooperate with those who take a sincere interest in AA?*

Meditation for the Day

God is always ready to pour his blessings into my heart in generous measure. But, as in the seed-sowing, the ground must be prepared before the seed is dropped in. It is my task to prepare the soil. It is God's to drop the seed. This preparation of the soil means many days of right living, choosing the right and avoiding the wrong.

Prayer for the Day

I pray that I may strive to make myself ready for the harvest that God has planted in my heart.

AA Thought for the Day

 We in AA must remember that we are offering something intangible. We are offering a psychological and spiritual program. We are not offering a medical program. If people need medical treatment, we call in a doctor. Our vital AA work begins when a person is physically able to receive it. *Am I willing to leave medical care to the doctors?*

Meditation for the Day

Every situation has two interpretations—my own and God's. I must try to handle each situation in the way I believe God would have it handled.

Prayer for the Day

I pray that I may make my day count somewhat for God. I pray that I may not spend it all selfishly.

AA Thought for the Day

First, people must be mentally able to receive the AA program. They must have made up their minds that they want to quit drinking, and they must be willing to do something about it. We must show them that we are their friends and really desire to help them. When we have their confidence, they will listen to us. Then, newcomers need the fellowship of other alcoholics who understand their problem. *Do I do my best to give mental help?*

Meditation for the Day

I seek conscious contact with God more and more each day and make God an abiding presence during the day. I must be conscious of his spirit helping me. All that is done without God's spirit is passing. All that is done with God's spirit is life eternal.

Prayer for the Day

I pray that I may be in the stream of eternal life.

AA Thought for the Day

 The fundamental basis of AA is belief in some Power greater than ourselves. This belief takes us off the center of the universe and allows us to transfer our problems to some power outside of ourselves. We turn to this Power for the strength we need to get sober and stay sober. We put our drinking problem in God's hands and leave it there. We stop trying to run our own life and seek to let God run it for us. *Do I do my best to give spiritual help?*

Meditation for the Day

Whenever I feel inadequate to any situation, I should realize that the feeling of inadequacy is disloyalty to God. I can just say to myself, *I know that God is with me and will help me to think and say and do the right thing.*

Prayer for the Day

I pray that I may be buoyed up by the feeling that God is with me.

AUGUST 6

AA Thought for the Day

Psychologists are turning to religion because just knowing about ourselves is not enough. We need the added dynamic of faith in a Power outside of ourselves. And clergy and rabbis are turning to psychology because faith is an act of the mind and will. Faith must be built largely on our own psychological experience. *Have I taken what I need from both psychology and religion when I live the AA way?*

Meditation for the Day

Refilling with the Spirit is something I need every day. For this refilling with the Spirit, I need these times of quiet communion, away, alone, without noise, without activity. From these times of communion I come forth with new power. When I am spiritually filled, there is no work too difficult for me.

Prayer for the Day

*I pray that I may be daily refilled
with the right spirit.*

AA Thought for the Day

 We in AA are offering an intangible thing, a psychological and spiritual program. It's a wonderful program. When we learn to turn to a Higher Power, with faith that that Power can give us the strength we need, we find peace of mind. We find new interests that make life worthwhile. It is the function of our AA program to produce modern miracles. *Do I consider the change in my life a modern miracle?*

Meditation for the Day

It is not a question of whether God can provide a shelter from the storm but of whether I seek the security of that shelter. Every fear, worry, or doubt is disloyalty to God. I must endeavor to trust God wholly. I practice saying, "All is going to be well." I say it to myself until I feel it deeply.

Prayer for the Day

I pray that I may feel deeply that all is well.
I pray that nothing will be able to move me from that deep conviction.

AA Thought for the Day

 For a while, we are going back to the Big Book, *Alcoholics Anonymous*, and picking out passages here and there, so that they may become fixed in our minds, a little at a time, day by day, as we go along. There is no substitute for reading the Big Book. It is our "bible." We should study it often. *Have I studied the Big Book faithfully?*

Meditation for the Day

All of life is a fluctuation between effort and rest. I need both every day. But effort is not truly effective until first I have had the proper preparation for it, by resting in a time of quiet meditation. The successful life is a proper balance between rest and effort.

Prayer for the Day

I pray that I may be ready to make the proper effort.
I pray that I may also recognize the
need for relaxation.

AA Thought for the Day

 "We have an allergy to alcohol. . . . We allergic types can never safely use alcohol in any form at all. We cannot be reconciled to a life without alcohol, unless we can experience an entire psychic change. Once this psychic change has occurred, we who seemed doomed, we who had so many problems that we despaired of ever solving them, find ourselves able to control our desire for alcohol." *Have I had a psychic change?*

Meditation for the Day

When I ask God to change me, I must at the same time fully trust him. If I do not fully trust him, God may answer my prayer as a rescuer does that of a drowning person who is putting up too much of a struggle. The rescuer must first render the person still more helpless, until he or she is wholly at the rescuer's mercy.

Prayer for the Day

I pray that I may put myself wholly
at the mercy of God.

AA Thought for the Day

 "We who have found this solution to our alcoholic problem, who are properly armed with the facts about ourselves, can generally win the entire confidence of another alcoholic. We who are making the approach to new prospects have had the same difficulty they have had. We obviously know what we are talking about. Our whole deportment shouts at new prospects that we are people with a real answer." *Am I a person with the real answer to the alcoholic problems of others?*

Meditation for the Day

For straying from the right way there is no cure except to keep so close to the thought of God that nothing, no other interest, can seriously come between myself and God.

Prayer for the Day

I pray that I may stay on God's side.

AA Thought for the Day

"Alcoholics usually have no idea why they take the first drink. Some drinkers have excuses with which they are satisfied, but in their hearts they really do not know why they do it. The truth is that at some point in their drinking they have passed into a state where the most powerful desire to stop drinking is of no avail." *Am I satisfied that I have passed my tolerance point for alcohol?*

Meditation for the Day

He who made the ordered world out of chaos and set the stars in their courses and made each plant to know its season, he can bring peace and order out of my private chaos if I will let him. I belong to God, and my affairs are his affairs and can be ordered by him if I am willing.

Prayer for the Day

I pray that I may be led out of disorder into order.

AUGUST 12

AA Thought for the Day

"The central fact of our lives today is the absolute certainty that our Creator has entered into our hearts and lives there in a way which is indeed miraculous. He has commenced to accomplish those things for us that we could never do for ourselves." *Have I let God come into my life?*

Meditation for the Day

The moment a thing seems wrong or a person's actions seem to not be what I think they should be, at that moment begins my obligation, my responsibility, to pray for those wrongs to be righted or that person to be changed. What is wrong in my surroundings or in the people I know? I can think about these matters and make them my responsibility—not to interfere but to pray for change.

Prayer for the Day

I pray that I may be a coworker with God.

AA Thought for the Day

"What seemed at first a flimsy reed has proved to be the loving and powerful hand of God. A new life has been given us, a design for living that really works. All of us establish in our own individual way our personal relationship with God." *Have I established my own relationship with God?*

Meditation for the Day

I make it a daily practice to review my character. Each day I try to see where God wants me to change. I plan how each fault can be best removed or each mistake corrected. Striving toward a better life is my ultimate goal.

Prayer for the Day

I pray that I may make real progress
toward a better life.

AA Thought for the Day

"Our drinking careers have been characterized by countless vain attempts to prove that we could drink like other people. This delusion that we are like other people has to be smashed. . . . There is no such thing as making a normal drinker out of an alcoholic." *Am I convinced that I can never drink again normally?*

Meditation for the Day

I should have life and have it more abundantly—spiritual, mental, physical, abundant life; joyous, powerful life. This I can have if I follow the right way. Not all people will accept from God the gift of an abundant life, a gift held out free to all. Not all people care to stretch out a hand and take it.

Prayer for the Day

I pray that I may hasten to accept the gift of abundant spiritual life.

AA Thought for the Day

 "Once an alcoholic, always an alcoholic. . . . If we have admitted we are alcoholics, we must have no reservations of any kind, nor any lurking notion that some day we will be immune to alcohol. . . . Parallel with sound reasoning, there inevitably runs some insanely trivial excuse for taking the first drink." *Have I given up all excuses for taking a drink?*

Meditation for the Day

"Where two or three are gathered in my name, there I am in the midst of them." When God finds two or three people in union who want only his will to be done, who want only to serve him, he has a plan that can be revealed to them. A union like this is miracle-working.

Prayer for the Day

I pray that I may be part of a unified group. I pray that I may contribute my share to its consecrated purpose.

AA Thought for the Day

"The alcoholic is absolutely unable to stop drinking on the basis of self-knowledge. We must admit we can do nothing about it ourselves. . . . Only spiritual principles will solve our problems. We are completely helpless apart from Divine help. Our defense against drinking must come from a Higher Power." *Have I accepted the spiritual answer and the program of action?*

Meditation for the Day

I must rest now until life, eternal life, flowing through my veins and heart and mind, calls me to action. Then glad work will follow. Tired work is never effective. I look to these quiet times of communion with God for rest, for peace, for cure.

Prayer for the Day

I pray that the peace I have found
will make me effective.

AA Thought for the Day

"We have to face the fact that we must find a spiritual basis of life—or else. Lack of power is our dilemma. We have to find a power by which we can live, and it has to be a power greater than ourselves." *Have I found that power by which I can live?*

Meditation for the Day

Sunshine is the laughter of nature, and I must live out in the sunshine. The sun and air are good medicine. Nature is a good nurse for tired bodies. God's grace is like the sunshine. I let my whole being be wrapped in the divine spirit.

Prayer for the Day

I pray that I may live in the sunshine of God's spirit. I pray that my mind and soul may be energized by it.

AA Thought for the Day

"As we were able to lay aside prejudice and express a willingness to believe in a Power greater than ourselves, we commenced to get results, even though it was impossible for any of us to fully define or comprehend that Power, which we call God. As soon as you can say that you do believe or are willing to believe, you are on your way." *Am I willing to depend on a Power that I cannot fully define or comprehend?*

Meditation for the Day

To realize God's presence I must surrender to his will in the small as well as in the big things of life. This makes God's guidance possible. Some things separate me from God—a false word, a fear-inspired failure, a harsh criticism, a stubborn resentment. A word of love, a selfless reconciliation, a kind act of helpfulness—these bring God closer.

Prayer for the Day

I pray that I may think and say and do the things that bring God closer to me.

AA Thought for the Day

"There is a wide variation in the way each one of us approaches and conceives of the Power greater than ourself. Whether we agree with a particular approach or conception seems to make little difference. . . . But in each case the belief in a Higher Power has accomplished the miraculous, the humanly impossible. There has come a revolutionary change in their way of living and thinking." *Has there been a revolutionary change in me?*

Meditation for the Day

Worship is consciousness of God's divine majesty. God brings to those who worship him a divine power, a divine love, and a divine healing. I only have to open my mind to him and try to absorb some of his divine spirit.

Prayer for the Day

I pray that I may worship God by sensing the eternal Spirit.

AA Thought for the Day

"When we see others solve their problems by simple reliance upon some Spirit of the universe, we have to stop doubting the power of God. Our ideas did not work, but the God-idea does. Deep down in every man, woman, and child is the fundamental idea of God. Faith in a Power greater than ourselves and miraculous demonstrations of that power in our lives are facts as old as the human race." *Am I willing to rely on the Spirit of the universe?*

Meditation for the Day

I should not dwell too much on the mistakes, faults, and failures of the past. I am done with shame and remorse and contempt for myself. With God's help, I can develop a new self-respect. Unless I respect myself, others will not respect me.

Prayer for the Day

I pray that I may keep picking myself up and making a fresh start each day.

AA Thought for the Day

"Who are you to say there is no God? This challenge comes to all of us. Are we capable of denying that there is a design and purpose in all of life as we know it? Or are we willing to admit that faith in some kind of Divine Principle is a part of our make-up, just as much as the feeling we have for a friend? We find a great Reality deep down within us, if we face ourselves as we really are." *Have I found the great Reality?*

Meditation for the Day

When I change to a new way of life, I leave many things behind me. It is only the earth-bound spirit that cannot soar. I must loosen somewhat the strands that tie myself to the earth. It is only the earthly desires that bind me.

Prayer for the Day

I pray that my spirit may soar in freedom.

AA Thought for the Day

 "Those who do not recover are people who are constitutionally incapable of being honest with themselves. There are such unfortunates. . . . There are those, too, who suffer from grave emotional and mental disorders, but many of them do recover, if they have the capacity to be honest." *Am I completely honest with myself and with other people?*

Meditation for the Day

It is not what happens to me so much as what use I make of it. I can take my sufferings, difficulties, and hardships and make use of them to help some unfortunate soul who is faced with the same troubles. Then something good will come out of my suffering, and the world will be a better place because of it.

Prayer for the Day

*I pray that some good may result
from my painful experiences.*

AA Thought for the Day

 "We who have accepted the AA principles have been faced with the necessity for a thorough personal housecleaning. We must face and be rid of the things in ourselves that have been blocking us. We therefore take a personal inventory. We take stock honestly. . . . Resentment is the number one offender, [and] . . . we must be free of anger." *Am I free of resentment and anger?*

Meditation for the Day

I keep in mind the goal I am striving for, the good life I am trying to attain. I do not let little things divert me from the path and will not be overcome by the small trials and vexations of each day. I try to see the purpose and plan to which all is leading.

Prayer for the Day

I pray that I may find the good life worth striving for.

AA Thought for the Day

 "When we saw our faults, we listed them. We placed them before us in black and white. We admitted our wrongs honestly and we were willing to set these matters straight. We reviewed our fears thoroughly. We asked God to remove our fears and we commenced to outgrow fear." *Am I facing my fears in the proper way?*

Meditation for the Day

I cling to the belief that all things are possible with God. If this belief is truly accepted, it is the ladder upon which a human soul can climb from the lowest pit of despair to the sublimest heights of peace of mind.

Prayer for the Day

I pray that I may believe deeply that all things are possible with God.

AA Thought for the Day

"Unless we discuss our defects with another person, we do not acquire enough humility, fearlessness, and honesty to really get the program. We must be entirely honest with somebody. . . . We pocket our pride and go to it. Once we have taken this step, withholding nothing, we can look the world in the eyes." *Have I discussed all my defects with another person?*

Meditation for the Day

When the world's cares and distractions intrude and my spirit becomes weak, I remember that God's spirit is always with me, to replenish and renew. Physical weariness and exhaustion make a time of rest and communion with God more necessary.

Prayer for the Day

I pray that I will not speak or act in the midst of emotional upheaval.

AA Thought for the Day

"We cannot divide our lives into compartments and keep some for ourselves. We must give all the compartments to God. We must say: 'My Creator, I am now willing that you should have all of me, good and bad. I pray that you now remove from me every single defect of character which stands in the way of my usefulness to you and my friends.'" *Am I still clinging to something that I will not let go?*

Meditation for the Day

The laws of nature cannot be changed and must be obeyed if I am to stay healthy. No exceptions will be made in my case. I must submit to the laws of nature or they will finally break me. If I am dishonest, impure, selfish, and unloving, I will not be living according to the laws of the spirit, and I will suffer the consequences.

Prayer for the Day

I pray that I may submit to the laws of nature and to the laws of God.

AA Thought for the Day

"We must be willing to make amends to all the people we have harmed. We must do the best we can to repair the damage done in the past. When we make amends, when we say: 'I'm sorry,' the person is sure at least to be impressed by our sincere desire to set right the wrong." *Have I made a sincere effort to make amends to the people I have harmed?*

Meditation for the Day

The grace of God cures disharmony and disorder in human relationships. As soon as I put my affairs, with their confusion and their difficulties, into God's hands, he begins to cure all the disharmony and disorder. God will do all that is necessary as painlessly as possible, but I must be willing to submit to his treatment, even if I cannot now see the meaning or purpose of it.

Prayer for the Day

I pray that I may accept whatever it takes to live a better life.

AA Thought for the Day

"We must continue to take personal inventory and continue to set right any new mistakes as we go along. We should grow in understanding and effectiveness. This is not an overnight matter; it should continue for our lifetime. Continue to watch for selfishness, dishonesty, resentment, and fear." *Am I checking my spiritual condition daily?*

Meditation for the Day

Happiness cannot be sought directly; it is a by-product of love and service. Service is a law of being. Little acts of love and encouragement, of service and help, erase the rough places of life and help to make the path smooth. If I do these things, I cannot help having my share of happiness.

Prayer for the Day

I pray that I will not grow weary in my attempts to do the right thing.

AA Thought for the Day

 "We cannot get along without prayer and meditation. On awakening, let us think about the twenty-four hours ahead. We consider our plans for the day. Before we begin, we ask God to direct our thinking. . . . We conclude this period of meditation with a prayer that we will be shown through the day what our next step is to be. The basis of all our prayers is: Thy will be done in me and through me today." *Am I sincere in my desire to do God's will today?*

Meditation for the Day

I have the gift of free will. When I choose the path of selfishness and greed and pride, I am refusing to accept God's spirit. When I choose the path of love and service, I accept God's spirit, and it flows into me and makes all things new.

Prayer for the Day

I pray that I may choose the right way.

AA Thought for the Day

"Practical experience shows that nothing will so much ensure immunity from drinking as extensive work with other alcoholics. Carry the message to other alcoholics. You can help when no one else can. You can secure their confidence when others fail. Life will take on a new meaning for you . . . this is an experience you must not miss." *Am I always ready and willing to help other alcoholics?*

Meditation for the Day

One secret of abundant living is the art of giving. The paradox of life is that the more I give, the more I have. If I lose my life in the service of others, I will save it. I must not let mean or selfish thoughts keep me from sharing this spirit.

Prayer for the Day

I pray that I may live to give.

AA Thought for the Day

"Call on new prospects while they are still jittery. They may be more receptive when depressed. See them alone if possible. Tell them enough about your drinking habits and experiences to encourage them to speak of themselves. If they wish to talk, let them do so. If they are not communicative, talk about the troubles liquor has caused you, being careful not to moralize or lecture." *Am I ready to talk about myself to new prospects?*

Meditation for the Day

I must try not to criticize, blame, scorn, or judge others when I am trying to help them. Effectiveness in helping others depends on controlling myself. I can go easy on them and be hard on myself and seek no personal recognition for what I am used by God to accomplish.

Prayer for the Day

I pray that I may always try to build up others instead of tearing them down.

SEPTEMBER

AA Thought for the Day

"Be careful not to brand new prospects as alcoholics. Let them draw their own conclusion. But talk to them about the hopelessness of alcoholism. Tell them exactly what happened to you and how you recovered. Stress the spiritual feature freely." *Do I hold back too much in speaking of the spiritual principles of the program?*

Meditation for the Day

"I will never leave you or forsake you." Down through the centuries, thousands have believed in God's constancy, untiringness, and unfailing love. Unless I want him to go, God will never leave me. He is always ready with power.

Prayer for the Day

I pray that I may have confidence in God's unfailing power.

AA Thought for the Day

"Outline the program of action to new prospects, explaining how you made a self-appraisal, how you straightened out your past, and why you are now endeavoring to help them. It is important for them to realize that your attempt to pass this on to them plays a vital part in your own recovery." *Can I tell the AA story to another alcoholic?*

Meditation for the Day

I should try to stand aside and let God work through me. God desires my obedient service and my loyalty to the ideals of the new life I am seeking. I will have true victory and real success, if I will put myself in the background and let God work through me.

Prayer for the Day

I pray that I will not interfere with the working of God's spirit in me and through me.

AA Thought for the Day

"Burn the idea into the consciousness of new prospects that they can get well, regardless of anyone else. Let no alcoholic say they cannot recover unless they have their family back. This just isn't so. Their recovery is not dependent upon other people. It is dependent on their own relationship to God." *Can I recognize all excuses made by a prospect?*

Meditation for the Day

As a child in its mother's arms, I stay sheltered in the understanding and love of God. God will relieve me of the weight of worry and care, misery and depression, want and woe, faintness and heartache, if I will let him. I lift up my eyes from earth's troubles and view the glory of the unseen God.

Prayer for the Day

I pray that I may leave my burdens in God's care.

AA Thought for the Day

"We must be careful never to show intolerance or hatred of drinking as an institution. Experience shows that such an attitude is not helpful to anyone. We are not fanatics or intolerant of people who can drink normally. Prospects are relieved when they find we are not witch burners." *Do I have tolerance for those who can drink normally?*

Meditation for the Day

I must try to keep calm in all circumstances and try not to fight back. I can call on the grace of God when I feel like retaliating. I can look to God for the inner strength to drop resentments that drag me down. If I am burdened by annoyances, I will lose my inward peace and the spirit of God will be shut out.

Prayer for the Day

I pray that I may do the things that make for peace.

AA Thought for the Day

One of the mottoes of AA is "First things first." This means that we should always keep in mind that alcohol is our number one problem. We must never let any other problem, whether of family, business, friends, or anything else, take precedence in our minds over our alcoholic problem. Anything that makes us forget our number one problem is dangerous to us. *Am I keeping sobriety in first place in my mind?*

Meditation for the Day

Spiritual progress is the law of my being. I see around me more and more of beauty and truth, knowledge, and power. Today I am stronger, braver, more loving as a result of what I did yesterday. This law of spiritual progress gives meaning and purpose to my life. I always expect better things ahead.

Prayer for the Day

I pray that I may be a part of the forces for good in the world.

AA Thought for the Day

 Another of the mottoes of AA is "Live and let live." This, of course, means tolerance of people who think differently than we do, whether they are in AA or outside of AA. We cannot afford the luxury of being intolerant or critical of other people. *Am I willing to live and let live?*

Meditation for the Day

Learning to know God as best I can draws the eternal life nearer to me. I can strive for what is real and of eternal value. The more I try to live in the consciousness of the unseen world, the gentler will be my passing into it when the time comes for me to go. This life on earth should be largely a preparation for the eternal life to come.

Prayer for the Day

I pray that I may live each day as though it were my last. I pray that I may live my life as though it were everlasting.

AA Thought for the Day

Another of the mottoes of AA is "Easy does it." This means that we just go along in AA doing the best we can and not getting steamed up over problems. We alcoholics are emotional people, and we have gone to excess in almost everything we have done. We have not known how to relax. Faith in a Higher Power can help us to learn to take it easy. *Have I learned to take it easy?*

Meditation for the Day

In my troubles and difficulties, I need nothing so much as a refuge, a place to relax, where I can lay down my burdens and get relief from my cares. I say to myself, *God is my refuge.* I say it until its truth sinks into my very soul. I say it until I know it and am sure of it.

Prayer for the Day

I pray that I may go each day to God as a refuge until fear goes and peace and security come.

AA Thought for the Day

 Once we have fully accepted the program we become humble about our achievement. We do not take too much credit for our sobriety. When we see another suffering alcoholic in the throes of alcoholism, we say to ourselves, *But for the grace of God, there go I.* We do not forget the kind of people we were. *Am I truly grateful for the grace of God?*

Meditation for the Day

A consciousness of God's presence as one who loves me makes all life different. The consciousness of God's love promotes the opening of my whole being to God. If I try to walk in God's love, I will have that peace which passes all understanding and a contentment that no one can take from me.

Prayer for the Day

I pray that I may walk in God's love.

AA Thought for the Day

When alcoholics are offered a life of sobriety by following the AA program, they will look at the prospect of living without alcohol and they will ask, "Am I going to be limited to a life where I will be stupid, boring, and glum, like some of the righteous people I see? I know I must get along without liquor, but how can I? Do you have a sufficient substitute?" *Have I found a more than sufficient substitute for drinking?*

Meditation for the Day

There can be no complete failure with God. Do I want to make the best of life? Then I must live as near as possible to God, the Master and Giver of all life. My reward for depending on God's strength will be sure.

Prayer for the Day

I pray that I may try to rely more fully on the grace of God.

AA Thought for the Day

 How can a person live without liquor and be happy? "The things we put in place of drinking are more than substitutes for it. One is the fellowship of Alcoholics Anonymous. In this company, you find release from care, boredom, and worry. . . . The most satisfactory years of your existence lie ahead. Among other AAs you will make lifelong friends. You will be bound to them with new and wonderful ties." *Does life mean something to me now?*

Meditation for the Day

It is not easy to serve both God and the world. It is difficult to claim the rewards of both. If I work for God, I must be prepared to sometimes stand apart from the world. If I am trying sincerely to serve God, I will have other and greater rewards than the world has to offer.

Prayer for the Day

I pray that I may be content with the rewards that come from serving God.

AA Thought for the Day

"You will be bound to the other AAs with new and wonderful ties, for you and they will escape disaster together and all will . . . journey to a better and more satisfactory life. You will know what it means to give of yourself that others may survive and rediscover life." *Have these things happened to me?*

Meditation for the Day

God manifests himself as power to resist temptation. God manifests himself as love— love and compassion for people and a willingness to help them. The grace of God manifests itself as peace of mind and serenity of character. I can have plenty of power, love, and serenity if I am willing to ask God for these things each day.

Prayer for the Day

I pray that I may see God's grace in the strength I receive, the love I know, and the peace I have.

AA Thought for the Day

"What draws newcomers to AA and gives them hope? They hear the stories of men and women whose experiences tally with their own. The expressions on the faces of the women, that undefinable something in the eyes of the men, the stimulating atmosphere of the AA clubroom, conspire to let them know that there is haven at last." *Have I found a real haven in AA?*

Meditation for the Day

"If your eye is healthy, your whole body will be full of light." The eye of the soul is the will. If my will is to do the will of God, to serve him with my life, to serve him by helping others, then truly shall my whole body be full of light.

Prayer for the Day

I pray that my eye may be healthy.

AA Thought for the Day

"No one is too discredited, nor has sunk too low, to be welcomed cordially into AA, if he or she means business. . . . The things that matter so much to some people no longer signify much to us." *Has AA taught me to be truly democratic?*

Meditation for the Day

When I call on God in prayer to help me overcome weakness, sorrow, pain, discord, and conflict, God never fails in some way to answer the appeal. When I am in need of strength for myself or for the help of some other person, I call on God in prayer. The power I need will come simply, naturally, and forcefully.

Prayer for the Day

I pray that I may bring peace where there is discord.

AA Thought for the Day

"How does AA grow? Some of us sell AA as we go about. Little clusters of twos and threes and fives keep springing up in different communities, through contact with the larger centers. Those of us who travel drop in at other groups as often as we can." *Am I doing all I can to spread AA wherever I go?*

Meditation for the Day

As I feel the existence of God and his power, I believe in him more and more. At the same time, I am more conscious of falling short of absolute trust in God. The soul's progress is an increasing belief, then a cry for more faith, a plea to conquer all unbelief, all lack of trust.

Prayer for the Day

I pray that with more power in my life will come more faith. I pray that I may come to trust God more each day.

AA Thought for the Day

"We all realize that we know only a little. God will constantly disclose more to all of us. Ask him in your morning meditations what you can do today for the person who is still sick. The answers will come, if your own house is in order. See to it that your relationship with God is right and great events will come to pass for you and countless others." *Am I always looking for ways of presenting the AA program?*

Meditation for the Day

"In quietness and in confidence shall be your strength." Confidence means to have faith in something. I could not live without confidence in others. When I have confidence in God's grace, I can face whatever comes. When I have confidence in God's love, I can be serene and at peace.

Prayer for the Day

I pray that I may find strength today in quietness.

AA Thought for the Day

The Twelve Steps seem to embody five principles: membership requirement, spiritual basis, personal inventory, restitution, and helping others. *Have I made all these Steps a part of me?*

Meditation for the Day

I live not only in time but also in eternity. If I abide with God and he abides with me, I may bring forth spiritual fruit that will last for eternity. Even here on earth I can live as though my real life were eternal.

Prayer for the Day

I pray that I may give freely
to all who ask my help.

AA Thought for the Day

Step One is, "We admitted we were powerless over alcohol—that our lives had become unmanageable." This is the membership requirement of AA We must admit that our lives are disturbed. We must accept that we are helpless before the power of alcohol and must surrender to the fact that we must stop drinking. *Is it difficult for me to admit that I am different from normal drinkers?*

Meditation for the Day

I can make a practical test. When I live the right way, things seem to work out well for me. If I disobey the laws of nature, the chances are that I will be unhealthy. If I disobey the spiritual and moral laws, the chances are that I will be unhappy. By following the laws of nature and the spiritual laws of honesty, purity, unselfishness, and love, I can expect to be reasonably healthy and happy.

Prayer for the Day

I pray that I may follow the path that leads to a better life.

AA Thought for the Day

Step Two is, "Came to believe that a Power greater than ourselves could restore us to sanity." *Step Three* is, "Made a decision to turn our will and our lives over to the care of God *as we understood Him.*" *Step Eleven* is, "Sought through prayer and meditation to improve our conscious contact with God *as we understood Him,* praying only for knowledge of His will for us and the power to carry that out." The fundamental basis of AA is a belief in some Power greater than ourselves. Let us not take this lightly. *Have I made the venture of belief in a Power greater than my own?*

Meditation for the Day

I dwell for a moment each day in a secret place, the place of communion with God, apart from the world, and by doing so receive strength to face the world. God is close to me in this quiet place of communion.

Prayer for the Day

I pray that I may renew my strength in quietness.

AA Thought for the Day

Let us continue with *Steps Two, Three,* and *Eleven.* We must turn to a Higher Power for help, because we are helpless ourselves. When we put our drinking problem in God's hands and leave it there, we have made the most important decision of our lives. From then on, we trust God for the strength to keep sober. *Am I trusting God for the strength to stay sober?*

Meditation for the Day

I feel at home in the world when I am in touch with the Divine Spirit of the universe. God wants me to have spiritual success and he intends that I have it. If I live my life as much as possible according to spiritual laws, I can expect my share of joy and peace, satisfaction and success.

Prayer for the Day

I pray that I will find happiness in doing the right thing.

AA Thought for the Day

Step Four is, "Made a searching and fearless moral inventory of ourselves." *Step Five* is, "Admitted to God, to ourselves, and to another human being the exact nature of our wrongs." *Step Six* is, "Were entirely ready to have God remove all these defects of character." *Step Seven* is, "Humbly asked Him to remove our shortcomings." *Step Ten* is, "Continued to take personal inventory and when we were wrong promptly admitted it." In taking a personal inventory, we have to be absolutely honest with ourselves and with other people. *Have I taken an honest inventory of myself?*

Meditation for the Day

It is easy to tell whether a thing is of God. If it is of God, it must be good. Honesty, purity, unselfishness, and love all lead to the abundant life.

Prayer for the Day

I pray that I may try to choose the best in life.

AA Thought for the Day

Let us continue with *Steps Four, Five, Six, Seven,* and *Ten.* In taking a personal inventory of ourselves, we must see ourselves as we really are. We must admit our faults openly and try to correct them. We must try to see where we have been dishonest, impure, selfish, and unloving. We do not do this once and forget it. We do it every day of our lives, as long as we live. *Am I taking a daily inventory of myself?*

Meditation for the Day

In improving my personal life, I have unseen help. I was not made so that I could see God. That would be too easy for me, and there would be no merit in obeying him. It takes an act of faith, a venture of belief, to realize the Unseen Power. Yet I have much evidence of God's existence in the strength that many people have received from the act of faith.

Prayer for the Day

I pray that my vision will not be blocked by intellectual pride.

AA Thought for the Day

Step Eight is, "Made a list of all persons we had harmed, and became willing to make amends to them all." *Step Nine* is, "Made direct amends to such people wherever possible, except when to do so would injure them or others." When we go to a person and say we are sorry, the reaction we get is almost invariably good. It takes courage to make the plunge, but the results more than justify it. *Have I done my best to make all the restitution possible?*

Meditation for the Day

A faith without joy is not entirely genuine. Faith in God should bring me a deep feeling of happiness and security, no matter what happens on the surface of my life. Each new day is an opportunity to serve God and improve my relationships with other people. This brings joy.

Prayer for the Day

I pray that my horizons may grow ever wide.

AA Thought for the Day

Step Twelve is, "Having had a spiritual awakening as the result of these steps, we tried to carry this message to alcoholics, and to practice these principles in all our affairs." Note that the basis of our effectiveness in carrying the message to others is the reality of our own spiritual awakening. If we have not changed, we cannot be used to change others. *Am I always ready to give away what I have learned in AA?*

Meditation for the Day

When I am faced with a problem beyond my strength, I must turn to God by an act of faith. It is that turning to God in each trying situation that I must cultivate. The turning may be one of glad thankfulness for God's grace in my life. Or my appeal to God may be a prayerful claiming of his strength to face a situation and finding that I have it when the time comes.

Prayer for the Day

*I pray that I may try to draw near to God
each day in prayer.*

AA Thought for the Day

 Let us continue with *Step Twelve*. We must practice these principles in all our affairs. This part of the Twelfth Step must not be overlooked. We do not just practice these principles in regard to our drinking problem. We practice them in *all* our affairs. We do not give one compartment of our lives to God and keep the other compartments to ourselves. We give our whole lives to God, and we try to do his will in every respect. *Do I carry the AA principles with me wherever I go?*

Meditation for the Day

"Lord, to whom shall we go but to you? You have the words of eternal life." The words of eternal life are the words from God that are heard in my heart and mind. They say to me in the stillness of my heart and mind and soul, "Do this and live."

Prayer for the Day

I pray that I may follow the inner urging of my soul.

AA Thought for the Day

"A spiritual experience is something that brings about a personality change. By surrendering our lives to God as we understand Him, we are changed. The nature of this change is evident in recovered alcoholics. This personality change is not necessarily in the nature of a sudden and spectacular upheaval. We do not need to acquire an immediate and overwhelming God-consciousness, followed at once by a vast change in feeling and outlook. In most cases, the change is gradual." *Do I see a gradual and continuing change in myself?*

Meditation for the Day

"Come to me, all who labor and are heavy-laden, and I will give you rest." For rest from the care of life, I can turn to God each day in prayer and communion. God's everlasting arms are underneath all and will support me.

Prayer for the Day

I pray that I am conscious of God's support.

AA Thought for the Day

"The acquiring of an immediate and overwhelming God-consciousness, resulting in a dramatic transformation, though frequent, is by no means the rule. Most of our spiritual experiences are of the educational variety, and they develop slowly over a period of time. Quite often friends of newcomers are aware of the difference long before they are themselves." *Is my outlook on life changing for the better?*

Meditation for the Day

I look at the world as my Father's house. I think of all people I meet as guests in my Father's house, to be treated with love and consideration. I look at myself as a servant in my Father's house, as a servant of all. I think of no work as beneath me.

Prayer for the Day

I pray that I may serve others
out of gratitude to God.

AA Thought for the Day

"What often takes place in a few months could seldom have been accomplished by years of self-discipline. With few exceptions, our members find that they have tapped an unsuspected inner resource which they presently identify with their own conception of a Power greater than themselves. Most of us think this awareness of a Power greater than ourselves the essence of spiritual experience." *Have I tapped that inner resource that can change my life?*

Meditation for the Day

God respects free will, the right of each person to accept or reject his miracle-working power. Only the sincere desire of the soul gives him the opportunity to bestow it.

Prayer for the Day

I pray that I may keep my mind open today to God's influence.

AA Thought for the Day

For the past two months we have been studying passages and Steps from the Big Book, *Alcoholics Anonymous*. Now why not read the book itself again? It is essential that the AA program become part of us. We cannot study the Big Book too much or too often. *How much of the Big Book have I thoroughly mastered?*

Meditation for the Day

Many things that I must accept in life are to be viewed not so much as something necessary for me personally, but as something to be experienced in order that I may share in the sufferings and problems of humanity. Unless I have been through the same experiences, I cannot understand other people or their makeup well enough to be able to help them.

Prayer for the Day

I pray that I may accept everything that comes my way as a part of life.

AA Thought for the Day

 We need to check up on ourselves periodically. Are we attending meetings regularly? Are we doing our share to carry the load? When there is something to be done, do we volunteer? Do we speak at meetings when asked, no matter how nervous we are? Do we accept each opportunity to do Twelfth Step work as a challenge? *Am I a good AA?*

Meditation for the Day

How do I get strength to be effective and to accept responsibility? By asking my Higher Power for the strength I need each day. For every task that is given me, there is also given me all the power necessary for the performance of that task. I do not need to hold back.

Prayer for the Day

I pray that I may accept every task as a challenge. I know I cannot wholly fail if God is with me.

AA Thought for the Day

The work of carrying on AA—leading group meetings, serving on committees, speaking before other groups, doing Twelfth Step work, spreading AA among the alcoholics of the community—all these things are done on a volunteer basis. If we don't volunteer to do something concrete for AA, the movement is that much less effective. *Am I doing my share for AA?*

Meditation for the Day

When I look to God for strength to face responsibility and am quiet before him, his healing touch causes the Divine Quiet to flow into my very being. When in weakness I cry to God, his touch brings healing, the renewal of my courage, and the power to meet every situation and be victorious.

Prayer for the Day

I pray that I will not falter or faint by the wayside, but renew my courage through prayer.

OCTOBER

AA Thought for the Day

 Self-consciousness is a form of pride. It is a fear that something may happen to us. What happens to us is not very important. The impression we make on others does not depend so much on the kind of a job we do as on our sincerity and honesty of purpose. *Am I holding back because I am afraid of not making a good impression?*

Meditation for the Day

I look to God for the true power that will make me effective. I see no other wholly dependable supply of strength. That is the secret of a truly effective life. And I, in my turn, will be used to help many others find effectiveness.

Prayer for the Day

I pray that I may feel that nothing good is too much for me if I look to God for help.

AA Thought for the Day

What makes an effective talk at an AA meeting? There is always a temptation to speak beyond our own experiences, in order to make a good impression. This is never effective. What does not come from the heart does not reach the heart. What comes from personal experience and a sincere desire to help the other person reaches the heart. *Do I speak for effect or with a deep desire to help?*

Meditation for the Day

"Thy will be done" must be my oft-repeated prayer. And in the willing of God's will there should be gladness. I should delight to do that will because when I do, all my life goes right and everything tends to work well for me in the long run.

Prayer for the Day

I pray that my will may be attuned to the will of God.

AA Thought for the Day

 How do we talk with new prospects? Are we always trying to dominate the conversation? Do we lay down the law and tell prospects what they will have to do? Do we judge them privately and feel that they have a small chance of making the program? Do we belittle them to ourselves? Or are we willing to bare our souls so as to get them talking about themselves? And then are we willing to be good listeners? *Will I do all I can to help them along the path to sobriety?*

Meditation for the Day

Peace is the result of righteousness. There is no peace in wrongdoing, but if I live the way God wants me to live, quietness and assurance follow.

Prayer for the Day

I pray that I may attain a state of true calmness.

AA Thought for the Day

 Are we critical of other members of AA or of new prospects? Do we ever say about other members, "I don't think they're sincere, I think they're bluffing, or I think they're taking a few drinks on the quiet?" Do we realize that our doubtful and skeptical attitudes are hurting those members, if only in our attitudes toward them, which they cannot help sensing? *Is my attitude always constructive and never destructive?*

Meditation for the Day

To be attracted toward God and a better life, I must be spirit-guided. To those who are spirit-guided there is strength and peace and calm to be found in communion with an unseen Lord. To those who believe in this God they cannot see but whose power they can feel, life has a meaning and purpose.

Prayer for the Day

I pray that I may be spirit-guided.

AA Thought for the Day

 Do we have any hard feelings about other group members or for any other AA group? Are we critical of the way a group member thinks or acts? Do we feel that another group is operating in the wrong way and do we broadcast it? Or do we realize that all AA members, no matter what their limitations, have something to offer and some good, however little, that they can do for AA? *Am I tolerant of people and groups?*

Meditation for the Day

All my movements, my goings and comings can be guided by the unseen Spirit. Every visit to help another, every unselfish effort to assist, can be blessed by that unseen Spirit. Every meeting of a need may not be a chance meeting but may have been planned by the unseen Spirit.

Prayer for the Day

I pray that I may be led by the spirit of God.

AA Thought for the Day

 Is it our desire to be big shots in AA? Do we always want to be up front in the limelight? Do we feel that nobody else can do as good a job as we can? Or are we willing to take seats in the back row once in awhile and let somebody else carry the ball? Part of the effectiveness of any AA group is the development of new members to carry on, to take over from the older members. Are we reluctant to give up authority? *Do I know that AA could carry on without me, if it had to?*

Meditation for the Day

I must cling to faith in God and in his power to change my ways. My faith in an unseen God will be rewarded by a useful and serviceable life. God will not fail to show me the way I should live, when in real gratitude and true humility I turn to him.

Prayer for the Day

I pray that I may be always willing to be changed for the better.

AA Thought for the Day

 Do we put too much reliance on any one member of the group? That is, do we make a tin god out of some person? Do we set that person on a pedestal? If we do, we are building our house on sand. All AA members have "clay feet." We are all only one drink away from a drunk, no matter how long we have been in AA. If that person we rely too much on should fail, where would we be? *Can I afford to be tipped over by the failure of my ideal?*

Meditation for the Day

I must always remember that I am weak and that God is strong. God knows all about my weakness. When I am weak, that is when God is strong to help me. If I trust God enough, my weakness will not matter. God is always strong to save.

Prayer for the Day

I pray that I may learn to lean on God's strength.

AA Thought for the Day

 There is such a thing as being too loyal to any one group. Do we feel put out when another group starts and some members of our group leave? Or do we send them out with our blessing? AA grows by the starting of new groups all the time. *Am I always ready to help new groups?*

Meditation for the Day

I pray—and keep praying until it brings peace and serenity and a feeling of communion with One who is near and ready to help. When I pray, there will flow into my heart such faith and love as is beyond the power of material things to give, and such peace as the world can neither give nor take away. And with God, I can have the tolerance to live and let live.

Prayer for the Day

*I pray that I may have true tolerance
and understanding.*

AA Thought for the Day

 Are we willing to be bored sometimes at meetings? Are we willing to hear the same thing over and over again? Are we willing to listen to a long blow-by-blow personal story, because it might help some new member? *Have I learned to take it?*

Meditation for the Day

God wants to draw me closer to him in the bonds of the spirit. He wants all people drawn closer to each other in the bonds of the spirit. God, the great Spirit of the universe, of which each of our own spirits is a small part, must want unity between himself and all of his children.

Prayer for the Day

I pray that I may be brought closer to unity with God and other people.

AA Thought for the Day

When new members come into our AA group, do we make a special effort to make them feel at home? Do we make it a habit to talk to all new members, or do we often leave that to someone else? When we see any members sitting alone, do we stay among our own special group of friends and leave them out in the cold? *Are all new AAs my responsibility?*

Meditation for the Day

I am God's servant. I serve him cheerfully and readily. Nobody likes a servant who avoids extra work or who complains about being called from one task to do one less enjoyable. A master would feel that he was being ill served by such a servant. I view my day's work in this light.

Prayer for the Day

I pray that I may be willing to go out of my way to be of service.

AA Thought for the Day

 How good a sponsor are we? When we bring new members to a meeting, do we feel that our responsibility has ended? If they don't show up for a meeting, do we look them up and find out whether there is a reason? Do we go out of our way to find out if there is anything more we can do to help? *Am I a good sponsor?*

Meditation for the Day

"First be reconciled to your brother, and then come and offer your gift to God." First I must get right with other people and then I can get right with God. If I hold a resentment against someone, I should pray for the one against whom I hold the resentment. I should put that person in God's hands and let God show him or her the way to live.

Prayer for the Day

I pray that I may see something good in every person, even one I dislike, and that I may let God develop the good in that person.

AA Thought for the Day

 Are we still on a "free ride" in AA? Are we all get and no give? Do we go to meetings and always sit in the back row and let the others do all the work? Do we think it's enough just because we're sober and can rest on our laurels? If so, we haven't gone very far in the program, nor are we getting nearly enough of what it has to offer. *Do I go in there and carry the ball?*

Meditation for the Day

I must do my small part every day in the spirit of service to God. Even when I am tempted to rest or let things go or to evade the issue, make it a habit to meet the issue squarely as a challenge and not to hold back.

Prayer for the Day

I pray that I may perform each task faithfully.

AA Thought for the Day

 AA work is one hundred percent voluntary. It depends on each and every one of our members to volunteer to do his or her share. Newcomers can sit on the sidelines until they have gotten over their nervousness and confusion. But the time inevitably comes when they have to speak up and volunteer to do their share in meetings and in Twelfth Step work. *Has my time come to volunteer?*

Meditation for the Day

God's kingdom on earth is growing slowly, like a seed in the ground. In the growth of his kingdom there is always progress among the few who are out ahead of the crowd. If I keep striving for something better, there can be no stagnation in my life.

Prayer for the Day

I pray that I may be willing to grow.

AA Thought for the Day

How big a part of our lives is AA? Is it just one of our activities and a small one at that? Do we only go to AA meetings now and then and some-times never go at all? Do we think of AA only occasionally? Are we reticent about mention-ing the subject of AA to people who might need help? Or does AA fill a large part of our lives? *Is AA the foundation on which I build my life?*

Meditation for the Day

I lay upon God my failures and mistakes and shortcomings. I do not dwell upon my failures, upon the fact that in the past I have been nearer a beast than an angel. I have a mediator between me and God—my growing faith.

Prayer for the Day

I pray that I may not let the beast in me hold me back from my spiritual destiny.

AA Thought for the Day

Are we deeply grateful to AA for what it has done for us in regaining our sobriety and opening up an entirely new life? AA has made it possible for us to carry on other interests. It has made a well-rounded life possible for us in school, in work, in play, and in hobbies of various kinds. But will we desert AA because of this? *Do I realize that I could have nothing worthwhile without AA?*

Meditation for the Day

If I live with God in that secret place of the spirit then I will have a feeling of being on the right road. I will have a deep sense of satisfaction. The world will have meaning and I will have a place in the world, work to do that counts in the eternal order of things. Many things will work for me and with me, as long as I feel I am on God's side.

Prayer for the Day

*I pray that I will not only work for now,
but also for eternity.*

AA Thought for the Day

 How seriously do we take our obligations to AA? Have we taken all of the good we can get out of it and then let our obligations slide? Or do we constantly feel a deep sense of loyalty to the whole AA movement? *Do I feel that I owe AA my loyalty and devotion?*

Meditation for the Day

If my heart is right, my world will be right. The beginning of all reform must be in myself. It's not what happens to me, it's how I take it. However restricted my circumstances, however little I may be able to remedy financial affairs, I can always turn to my inward self and, seeing something not in order there, seek to right it. As I improve myself, my outward circumstances will change for the better.

Prayer for the Day

I pray that the hidden power within me
may be released.

AA Thought for the Day

 What are we going to do *today* for AA? Is there someone we should call up on the telephone or someone we should go to see? Is there an opportunity somewhere to advance the work of AA that we have been putting off or neglecting? If so, will we do it *today?* Will we be done with procrastination and do what we have to do today? *Do I feel that AA depends partly on me today?*

Meditation for the Day

Today I look upward toward God, not downward toward myself. I look away from unpleasant surroundings, from lack of beauty, from the imperfections in myself and in those around me. In my unrest, behold God's calmness; in my impatience, God's patience; in my limitations, God's perfection.

Prayer for the Day

I pray that I may see infinite possibilities for spiritual growth.

AA Thought for the Day

Have we gotten over most of our sensitiveness, our feelings that are too easily hurt, and our just plain laziness and self-satisfaction? Is our own comfort more important to us than doing the things that need to be done? Have we reached the point where what happens to us is not so important? *Am I willing to give all of myself whenever necessary?*

Meditation for the Day

Not until I have failed can I learn true humility. Humility arises from a deep sense of gratitude to God for giving me the strength to rise above past failures. Humility is not inconsistent with self-respect. The true person has self-respect and the respect of others and yet is humble.

Prayer for the Day

I pray that I may be truly humble
and yet have self-respect.

AA Thought for the Day

Do we realize that we do not know how much time we have left? It may be later than we think. Are we going to do the things that we know we should do before our time runs out? By the way, what is our purpose for the rest of our lives? *Am I going to make what time I have left count for AA?*

Meditation for the Day

I can believe that somehow the cry of the human soul is never unheard by God. It may be that God hears the cry, even if I fail to notice God's response to it. One thing I can believe is that the grace of God is always available for every human being who sincerely calls for help.

Prayer for the Day

I pray that I may trust God to answer my prayer as he sees fit.

AA Thought for the Day

 For the past few weeks we have been asking ourselves some searching questions. We have not been able to answer them all as we would like. But the usefulness and effectiveness of our lives will depend on the right answers to these questions. It all boils down to this: we owe a deep debt to AA and to the grace of God. Are we going to do all we can to repay that debt? *What am I going to do about it?*

Meditation for the Day

I continue to pray, "Not my will but Thy will be done." It may not turn out the way I want it to, but it will be the best way in the long run, because it is God's way. If I decide to accept whatever happens as God's will for myself, whatever it may be, my burdens will be lighter. I try to see in all things some fulfillment of the divine intent.

Prayer for the Day

*I pray that I may see
the working out of God's will in my life.*

AA Thought for the Day

We understand ourselves more than we ever did before. We have learned what was the matter with us and we know now a lot of what makes us tick. We will never be alone again. We are just one of many who have the illness of alcoholism and one of many who have learned what to do about it. We are not square pegs in round holes. We seem to have found our right place in the world. *Am I beginning to understand myself?*

Meditation for the Day

"Behold, I stand at the door and knock; if anyone hears my voice and opens the door, I will come in to him and eat with him, and he with me." The knocking of God's spirit, asking to come into my life, is not due to any merit of mine, though it is in response to the longing of my heart.

Prayer for the Day

I pray that I may let God's spirit
come into my heart.

AA Thought for the Day

We are content to face the rest of our lives without alcohol. No death of a dear one, no great calamity in any area of our lives would justify drinking. Even if we were on some desert isle, far from the rest of the world, but not far from God, we would never feel it right to drink. For us, alcohol is out—period. *Am I fully resigned to this fact?*

Meditation for the Day

Day by day I should slowly build up an unshakable faith in a Higher Power and in that Power's ability to give me all the help I need. By having these quiet times each morning, I start each day with a renewing of my faith, until it becomes almost a part of me and is a strong habit.

Prayer for the Day

I pray that I may build a house in my soul
for the spirit of God to dwell.

AA Thought for the Day

We have learned how to be honest. What a relief! No more ducking or dodging. No more tall tales. No more pretending to be what we are not. Our cards are on the table for all the world to see. *Am I really honest?*

Meditation for the Day

Though it may seem a paradox, I must believe in spiritual forces that I cannot see more than in material things that I can see, if I am going to truly live. In the last analysis, the universe consists more of thought or mathematical formulas than it does of matter as I understand it.

Prayer for the Day

I pray that I may believe in the unseen.

AA Thought for the Day

We have turned to a Power greater than ourselves. Thank God, we are no longer at the center of the universe. All the world does not revolve around us any longer. We are among many. We are on the Way and the whole power of the universe is behind us when we do the right thing. We do not have to depend entirely on ourselves any longer. With God, we can face anything. *Is my life in the hands of God?*

Meditation for the Day

I can have a new life of power. But only in close contact with the grace of God is its power realized. In order to realize it and benefit from it, I must have daily quiet communion with God, so that the power of his grace will come unhindered into my soul.

Prayer for the Day

I pray that I may be kept from evil
by the grace of God.

AA Thought for the Day

 Now is ours. We can do what we want with it. We own it, for better or worse. What we do now, in this present moment, is what makes up our lives. Our whole lives are only a succession of nows. We will take this moment, which has been given to us by the grace of God, and we will do something with it. What we do with each now will make us or break us. *Am I living in the now?*

Meditation for the Day

I can never become entirely unselfish. But I can come to realize that I am not at the center of the universe and that everything does not revolve around me at the center.

Prayer for the Day

I pray that I may achieve the right perspective on my position in the world.

AA Thought for the Day

 We have AA meetings to go to, thank God. Where would we go without them? Where would we be without them? Where would we find the sympathy, the understanding, the fellowship, the companionship? We have found the place where we belong. *Do I thank God every day for the AA fellowship?*

Meditation for the Day

I must walk all the way with another person and with God. I must make a good companion of God, by praying to him often during the day. I do not let my contact with him be broken for too long a period.

Prayer for the Day

I pray that I may keep my feet upon the path that leads upward.

AA Thought for the Day

We can help other alcoholics. We are of some use in the world. We have a purpose in life. We are worth something at last. Our lives have direction and meaning. All that feeling of futility is gone. We can do something worthwhile. This is our opportunity and our destiny. *Will I give as much of my life as I can to AA?*

Meditation for the Day

I have a battle to win, the battle between the material view of life and the spiritual view. Something must guide my life. Will it be wealth, pride, selfishness, and greed, or will it be faith, honesty, purity, unselfishness, love, and service?

Prayer for the Day

*I pray that I may choose the good
and resist the evil.*

AA Thought for the Day

What other rewards have come to us as a result of our new way of living? Each one of us can answer this question in many ways. Our relationships are on an entirely new plane. The total selfishness is gone and more cooperation has taken its place. Understanding has taken the place of misunderstanding, accusations, bickering, and resentment. *Have I come home?*

Meditation for the Day

I can bow to God's will in anticipation of the thing happening that will, in the long run, be the best for all concerned. It may not always seem the best thing at the present time, but I only need to believe that if I trust him and accept whatever happens as his will in a spirit of faith, everything will work out for the best in the end.

Prayer for the Day

I pray that I will not ask to see the distant scene.

AA Thought for the Day

Our relationships with our families have greatly improved. Those who saw us drunk and were ashamed, those who turned away in fear and even loathing, have seen us sober and like us; they have turned to us in confidence and trust. They have given us a chance for companionship that we had completely missed. *Have I found something that I had lost?*

Meditation for the Day

True measure of success in life is the measure of spiritual progress that I have revealed in my life. Others should be able to see a demonstration of God's will in my life.

Prayer for the Day

I pray that I may so live that others will see in me something of the working out of the will of God.

AA Thought for the Day

Our idea of friendship has changed. Friends are no longer people whom we can use for our own pleasure or profit. Friends are people who understand us and whom we understand, whom we can help and who can help us to live better lives. We have learned not to hold back and wait for friends to come to us, but to go halfway and to be met halfway, openly and freely. *Does friendship have a new meaning for me?*

Meditation for the Day

There is a time for everything. I waste my energy in trying to get things before I am ready to have them, before I have earned the right to receive them. I can believe that all my life is a preparation for something better to come when I have earned the right to it. I can believe that God has a plan for my life and that this plan will work out in the fullness of time.

Prayer for the Day

I pray that I will not expect things until I have earned the right to have them.

AA Thought for the Day

 Life has fallen into place. The pieces of the jigsaw puzzle have found their correct position. Life is whole, all of one piece. We have found where we belong. We do not vainly wish for things we cannot have. We have "the serenity to accept the things I cannot change, the courage to change the things I can, and the wisdom to know the difference." *Have I found contentment in AA?*

Meditation for the Day

Everyone has an inner consciousness that tells of God, an inner voice that speaks to the heart. It is a voice that speaks to me intimately, personally, in a time of quiet meditation. As the Big Book puts it: "Deep down in every man, woman, and child is the fundamental idea of God. We can find the Great Reality deep down within us. And when we find it, it changes our whole attitude toward life."

Prayer for the Day

I pray that I will not turn a deaf ear
to the urging of my conscience.

NOVEMBER

AA Thought for the Day

We have hope—that magic thing that we had lost or misplaced. The future looks dark no more. We do not even look at it, except when necessary to make plans. We try to let the future take care of itself. Hope is justified by many right nows, by the rightness of the present. Nothing can happen to us that God does not will for us. *Do I have hope?*

Meditation for the Day

Faith is the messenger that bears my prayers to God. Prayer can be sure of some response from God. So I should pray to God with faith and trust and gratitude.

Prayer for the Day

I pray that I may be content with whatever form the response to my prayers takes.

AA Thought for the Day

 We have faith—that thing that makes the world seem right. That thing that makes sense at last. That awareness of the Divine Principle in the universe that holds it all together and gives it unity and purpose and goodness and meaning. It is all one glorious whole, because God is holding it together. *Do I have faith?*

Meditation for the Day

I keep myself like an empty vessel for God to fill. I keep pouring out myself to help others so that God can keep filling me up with his spirit. The more I give, the more I will have for myself. God will see that I am kept filled as long as I am giving to others. But if I selfishly try to keep all for myself, I am soon blocked off from God, my source of supply, and I will become stagnant. To be clear, a lake must have an inflow and an outflow.

Prayer for the Day

I pray that I may keep pouring out what I receive.

AA Thought for the Day

 We have charity, another word for love. That right kind of love that is not selfish passion but an unselfish, outgoing desire to help other people. To do what is best for the other person, to put what is best for him or her above our own desires. To put God first, the other person second, and ourselves last. What we do for others may be written somewhere in eternity. *Do I have charity?*

Meditation for the Day

"Ask whatever you will, and it shall be done for you." God has unlimited power. There is no limit to what his power can do in human hearts. But I must will to have God's power and I must ask God for it. God's power is blocked off from me by my indifference to it.

Prayer for the Day

I pray that I may will to have God's power.

AA Thought for the Day

We can do things that we never did before. Liquor took away our initiative and our ambition. We couldn't get up the steam to start anything. We let things slide. When we were drunk, we were too inert to even comb our hair. We have the urge to create something, that creative urge that was completely stifled by alcohol. We are free to achieve again. *Have I recovered my initiative?*

Meditation for the Day

"In Thy presence there is fullness of joy; in Thy right hand are pleasures forever." Seeking pleasure does not bring happiness in the long run, only disillusionment. Happiness is a by-product of living the right kind of life.

Prayer for the Day

I pray that I will not always seek pleasure as a goal. I pray that I may be content with the happiness that comes when I do the right thing.

AA Thought for the Day

 What are some of the things we have lost? Each one of us can answer this question in many ways. We have lost much of our fear. It used to control us; it was our master. It paralyzed our efforts. Fear always got us down. It made us introverts, ingrown persons. When fear was replaced by faith, we got well. *Have I lost some of my fears?*

Meditation for the Day

The world would sooner be brought close to God, his will would sooner be done on earth, if all who acknowledge him gave themselves unreservedly to being used by him. If I live each day for God and allow God to work through me, then the world is drawn much closer to God.

Prayer for the Day

I pray that I may be used as a channel
to express the Divine Love.

AA Thought for the Day

 We were nervous wrecks from fear and worry. We were tied-up bundles of nerves. We had a fear of failure, of the future, of sickness, of hangovers, of suicide. We had a wrong set of ideas and attitudes. When AA told us to surrender these fears and worries to a Higher Power, we did so. We now try to think faith instead of fear. *Have I put faith in place of fear?*

Meditation for the Day

Spiritual power is God in action. God can act only through human beings. Whenever I, however weak I may be, allow God to act through me, then all I think and say and do is spiritually powerful. It is not I alone who produces a change in the lives of others!

Prayer for the Day

I pray that I may get rid of those blocks which keep God's power from me.

AA Thought for the Day

 We have lost many of our resentments. We have found that getting even with people doesn't do any good. Trying to get revenge, instead of making us feel better, leaves us frustrated and cheated. Instead of punishing our enemies, we've only hurt our own peace of mind. It does not pay to nurse a grudge; it hurts us more than anyone else. *Have I lost my resentments?*

Meditation for the Day

It is not so much me as the grace of God that is in me that helps those around me. If I want to help even those I dislike, I have to make sure that there is nothing in me to block the way, to keep God's grace from using me. My own pride and selfishness are the greatest blocks. If I keep those out of the way then God's grace will flow through me into the lives of others.

Prayer for the Day

I pray that all who come in contact with me will feel better for it.

AA Thought for the Day

 We have lost much of our inferiority complex. We were always trying to escape from life. We did not want to face reality. We were full of self-pity. We were constantly sorry for ourselves. We tried to avoid all responsibilities. AA showed us how to get over our feelings of inferiority. It made us want to accept responsibility again. *Have I lost my inferiority complex?*

Meditation for the Day

I should forget those things that are behind me and press onward toward something better. I can believe that God has forgiven me for all my past sins, provided I am honestly trying to live today the way I believe he wants me to live. I can start today with a clean slate and go forward with confidence toward the goal that has been set before me.

Prayer for the Day

I pray that I may start today with a light heart and a new confidence.

AA Thought for the Day

We used to take a negative view of almost everything. There seemed to be very little good in the world, but lots of hypocrisy and sham. People could not be trusted. Those were our general attitudes toward life. Now we are more positive. We believe in people and in their capabilities. There is much love and truth and honesty in the world. *Am I less negative and more positive?*

Meditation for the Day

I think of God as a Great Friend and try to realize the wonder of that friendship. When I give God not only worship, obedience, and allegiance, but also close companionship, then he becomes my friend, even as I am his. I can feel that he and I are working together. My prayers become more real to me when I feel that God counts on my friendship and I count on his.

Prayer for the Day

I pray that I may think of God as my Friend.

AA Thought for the Day

 The world used to revolve around us. We cared more about ourselves, our own needs and desires, our own pleasures, our own way, than we did about the whole rest of the world. What happened to us was more important than anything else we could think of. We were selfishly trying to be happy, and therefore we were unhappy most of the time. We have found that selfishly seeking pleasure does not bring true happiness. *Am I less self-centered?*

Meditation for the Day

When something happens to upset me and I am discouraged, I try to feel that life's difficulties and troubles are not intended to stop my progress in the spiritual life but to test my strength and to increase my determination to keep going. Whatever it is that must be met, I am to either overcome it or use it.

Prayer for the Day

I pray that I may know that there can be no failure with God.

AA Thought for the Day

 AA has taught us to be more outgoing, to seek friendship by going at least halfway, to have a sincere desire to help. We have more self-respect now that we have less sensitiveness. We have found that the only way to live comfortably with ourselves is to take a real interest in others. *Do I realize that I am not so important after all?*

Meditation for the Day

As I look back over my life, it is not too difficult to believe that what I went through was for a purpose, to prepare me for some valuable work in life. Life is like the pattern of a mosaic. Each thing that happened to me is like one tiny stone in the mosaic, and each tiny stone fits into the perfected pattern of the mosaic of my life, which has been designed by God.

Prayer for the Day

I pray that I may trust the Designer.

AA Thought for the Day

 We used to run people down all the time. We realize now that it was because we wanted unconsciously to build ourselves up. We were envious of people who lived normal lives. We couldn't understand why we couldn't be like them. And so we ran them down. We were always looking for faults in the other person. We have found that we can never make a person any better by criticism. *Am I less critical of people?*

Meditation for the Day

I must admit my helplessness before my prayer for help will be heard by God. My own need must be recognized before I can ask God for the strength to meet that need. But once that need is recognized, my prayer is heard above all the music of heaven.

Prayer for the Day

I pray that I may send my voiceless cry for help out into the void. I pray that I may feel certain that it will be heard somewhere, somehow.

AA Thought for the Day

 Who are we to judge other people? Until we came into AA, our lives could be called failures. We made all the mistakes one could make. We took all the wrong roads there were to take. On the basis of our records, are we fit to be a judge of other people? *Am I less harsh in my judgment of people?*

Meditation for the Day

In times of meditation, I seem to hear, "Come to me, all who labor and are heavy-laden, and I will give you rest." Again and again I hear God saying this to me. "Come to me" for the solution of every problem, for the overcoming of every temptation, for the calming of every fear, for all needs physical, mental, or spiritual, but mostly "come to me" for the strength to live with peace of mind and the power to be useful and effective.

Prayer for the Day

I pray that I may go to God today.

AA Thought for the Day

 A better way than judging people is to look for all the good in them. If we look hard enough and long enough, we ought to be able to find some good in every person. In AA we learned that our job was to try to bring out the good, not criticize the bad. People are not converted by criticism. *Do I look for the good in people?*

Meditation for the Day

In times of quiet meditation I can seek for God's guidance, for the revealing of God's plan for my day. Then I can live this day according to that guidance. Many people are not making of their lives what God meant them to be, and so they are unhappy. They have missed the design for their lives.

Prayer for the Day

I pray that I may have the sense of divine intent in what I do today.

AA Thought for the Day

We are less sensitive and our feelings are less easily hurt. We no longer take ourselves so seriously. What happens to us now is not so important. One cause of our drinking was that we couldn't take it, so we escaped the unpleasant situation. We have learned to take it on the chin if necessary and smile. *Am I less sensitive?*

Meditation for the Day

God's miracle-working power is as manifest today as it was in the past. It still works miracles of change in lives and miracles of healing in twisted minds. When I trust wholly in God and leave to him the choosing of the day and hour, God's miracle-working power manifests in my life. So I can trust in God and have boundless faith in his power to make me whole again, whenever he chooses.

Prayer for the Day

I pray that I may feel sure that there is nothing that God cannot accomplish in changing my life.

AA Thought for the Day

We were always at war with ourselves. We were doing things that we did not want to do. We were waking up in strange places and wondering how we got there. We were full of recklessness when we were drunk and full of remorse when we were sober. Our lives didn't make sense. They were full of broken resolves and frustrated hopes and plans. We were getting nowhere fast. *Have I gotten rid of inner conflicts?*

Meditation for the Day

"Where two or three are gathered in my name, there am I in the midst of them." When two or three consecrated souls are together at a meeting place, the spirit of God is there to help and guide them. Where any sincere group of people are together, reverently seeking the help of God, his power and his spirit are there to inspire them.

Prayer for the Day

I pray that I may feel the strength
of a consecrated group.

AA Thought for the Day

 When we were drinking, our bad personality was in control. We did things when we were drunk that we would never do when we were sober. When we sobered up, we became different people. But we drink again, and so we are back and forth, always in conflict with our other selves. We become unified by giving ourselves wholeheartedly to AA and to sobriety. *Have I become unified?*

Meditation for the Day

"Well done, good and faithful servant. Enter into the joy of Thy Lord." These words are for many ordinary people whom the world may pass by, not recognizing them. Not to the famous, the proud, the wealthy are these words spoken, but to the quiet followers who serve God unobtrusively yet faithfully, who bear their crosses bravely and put a smiling face to the world.

Prayer for the Day

I pray that I will not desire the world's applause.

AA Thought for the Day

 We were always putting things off till tomorrow, and as a result they never got done. Under the influence of alcohol, we had grandiose plans. When we were sober we were too busy getting over our hangovers to start anything. In AA we have learned that it's better to make a mistake once in awhile than to never do anything at all. *Have I learned to do it now?*

Meditation for the Day

I should not hide my light under a bushel. The glory of God shines in the beauty of my character. It is in me, even though I can realize it only in part. The glory of God is too dazzling for mortals to see fully on earth. But some of this glory is in me when I try to reflect that light in my life.

Prayer for the Day

I pray that I may try to be a reflection of the Divine Light.

AA Thought for the Day

Putting sex in its proper place in our lives is one of the rewards that has come to us as a result of our new way of living. The Big Book says that many of us needed an overhauling there. "We remembered always that our sex powers were God-given and therefore good, neither to be used lightly or selfishly, nor to be despised or loathed." We can ask God to mold our ideals and to help us to live up to them. *Have I gotten my sex life under proper control?*

Meditation for the Day

I try to raise my thoughts from the depths of the sordid and mean and impure things of the earth to the heights of goodness and decency and beauty. I train my insight by trying to take the higher view. I train it more and more until distant heights become more familiar.

Prayer for the Day

I pray that I will not keep my eyes forever downcast. I pray that I may set my sights on higher things.

AA Thought for the Day

 We no longer try to escape life through alcoholism. Drinking built up an unreal world for us, and we tried to live in it. But in the morning light the real life was back again, and facing it was harder than ever, because we had fewer resources with which to meet it. AA taught us to not run away but to face reality. *Have I given up trying to escape life?*

Meditation for the Day

In these times of quiet meditation, I try more and more to set my hopes on the grace of God. Know that whatever the future may hold, it will hold more and more of good. I do not set all hopes and desires on material things. There is weariness in an abundance of things. I set my hopes on spiritual things so that I may grow spiritually and learn to rely on God's power more and more.

Prayer for the Day

I pray that I may not be overwhelmed by material things.

AA Thought for the Day

 We no longer waste money, but try to put it to good use. When we were drunk, we threw money around like we really had it. It gave us a feeling of importance—we felt like millionaires for a day. But the morning after, with an empty wallet, was a sad awakening. *How could I have been such a fool?* When we are sober, we spend our money as it should be spent. *Am I making good use of my money?*

Meditation for the Day

I was meant to be at home and comfortable in the world, not to live a life of quiet desperation. I let others see that I am comfortable, and seeing it, know that it springs from me trust in a Higher Power.

Prayer for the Day

I pray that I may be more comfortable
in my way of living.

AA Thought for the Day

 We have gotten rid of most of our boredom. One of the most difficult things that a new member of AA has to understand is how to stay sober and not be bored. Drinking was always the answer to all kinds of boring people or boring situations. Sobriety should give us so many new interests in life that we shouldn't have time to be bored. *Have I gotten rid of the fear of being bored?*

Meditation for the Day

Charity means to care enough about other people to really want to do something for them. A smile, a word of encouragement, a word of love goes winged on its way, simple though it may seem. Boredom comes from thinking too much about myself.

Prayer for the Day

I pray that my day may be brightened
by some little act of charity.

AA Thought for the Day

Many of us alcoholics use the excuse of not being able to do something perfectly to enable us to do nothing at all. We pretend to be perfectionists. In AA we set our goals high, but that does not prevent us from trying. The mere fact that we will never fully reach these goals does not prevent us from doing the best we can. *Have I stopped hiding behind the smoke screen of perfectionism?*

Meditation for the Day

"In the world you have tribulation; but be of good cheer, I have overcome the world." I can be undefeated and untouched by failure and all its power by letting my spirit overcome the world; rise above earth's turmoil into the secret chamber of perfect peace and confidence.

Prayer for the Day

I pray that I may have confidence
and be of good cheer.

AA Thought for the Day

 Instead of pretending to be perfectionists, in AA we are content if we are making progress. The main thing is to be growing. In AA we are willing to make mistakes and to stumble, provided we are always stumbling forward. We are not so interested in what we are as in what we are becoming. *Am I making progress?*

Meditation for the Day

Each new day brings an opportunity to do some little thing that will help to make a better world, that will bring God's kingdom a little nearer to being realized on earth. I take each day's happenings as opportunities for something I can do for God. In that spirit, a blessing will attend all that I do.

Prayer for the Day

I pray that I may be content
with doing small things as long as they are right.

AA Thought for the Day

When we were drinking, we were secretly full of jealousy and envy of those people who could drink normally. We pretended to ourselves that we were as good as they were, but we knew it wasn't so. Now we don't have to be envious anymore. We're content with what we have earned by our efforts to live the right way. More power to those who have what we don't have. At least we're trying. *Have I gotten rid of the poison of envy?*

Meditation for the Day

"My soul is restless till it finds its rest in you." I yearn to realize a peace, a rest, a satisfaction that I have never found in the world or its pursuits. Some are not conscious of their need and shut the doors of their spirits against the spirit of God. They are unable to have true peace.

Prayer for the Day

I pray that my soul may find its rest in God.

AA Thought for the Day

 We have gotten rid of our fears, resentments, inferiority complexes, negative points of view, self-centeredness, criticism of others, oversensitiveness, inner conflicts, the habits of procrastination, undisciplined sex, wasting money, boredom, false perfectionism, jealousy, and envy of others. *Am I ready to go forward in the new life?*

Meditation for the Day

"He that has eyes to see, let him see." I pray for a seeing eye, to see the purpose of God in everything good. I pray for enough faith to see God's care in his dealings with me. I try to see how he has brought me safely through my past life so that now I can be of use in the world.

Prayer for the Day

I pray that with the eye of faith
I may see God's purpose everywhere.

AA Thought for the Day

 The way of AA is the way of sobriety, fellowship, service, and faith. The first and greatest to us is sobriety. We could not have the others if we did not have sobriety. We all come to AA to get sober, and we stay to help others get sober. We are looking for sobriety first, last, and all the time. *Am I on the AA way?*

Meditation for the Day

I start out wanting my own way. I want my will to be satisfied. I take and I do not give. Gradually I find that I am not happy when I am selfish, so I begin to make allowances for other people's wills. But this again does not give me full happiness, and I begin to see that the only way to be truly happy is to try to do God's will.

Prayer for the Day

I pray that I may be guided today
to find God's will for me.

AA Thought for the Day

 We believe that AA is the most successful and happiest way to sobriety. And yet AA is, of course, not completely successful. Some are unable to achieve sobriety, and some slip back into alcoholism after a time of sobriety. *Am I deeply grateful to have found AA?*

Meditation for the Day

Gratitude to God is the theme of Thanksgiving Day. The pilgrims gathered to give thanks to God for their harvest, which was pitifully small. When I look around at all the things I have today, how can I help being grateful to God?

Prayer for the Day

I pray that I will not forget where I might be but for the grace of God.

AA Thought for the Day

Many alcoholics have tried drinking after a period of sobriety from a few days to a few years and no one that we know of has been successful in becoming a normal drinker. *Do I know that I'm not an exception to this rule?*

Meditation for the Day

"We are gathered together in Thy name." First, we are gathered together, bound by a common loyalty to God and to each other. Then, when this condition has been fulfilled, God is present with us. Then, when God is there and one with us, we voice a common prayer. Then it follows that our prayer will be answered according to God's will. When our prayer is answered, we are bound together in a lasting fellowship of the spirit.

Prayer for the Day

I pray that I may be loyal to God and to others.

AA Thought for the Day

 It has been said that slips are premeditated drunks, because we have to think about taking a drink before we actually take one. The thought always comes before the act. It is suggested that people should always get in touch with an AA before taking that first drink. And yet the thoughts that come before taking a drink are often largely subconscious. *Am I on guard against wrong thinking?*

Meditation for the Day

I can get away from the misunderstanding of others by retreating into my own place of meditation. But from myself, from my sense of failure, my weakness, my shortcomings, I can only flee to the eternal God, my refuge, until the immensity of his spirit envelops my spirit and it loses its smallness and weakness and comes into harmony again with his spirit.

Prayer for the Day

*I pray that I may lose my limitations
in the immensity of God's love.*

DECEMBER

AA Thought for the Day

 When we are asleep, some of us dream about being drunk even after several years of sobriety. Our subconscious minds have been thoroughly conditioned by our alcoholic way of thinking, and it is doubtful that they will ever become entirely free of such thoughts during our lifetime. But when our conscious minds are fully conditioned against drinking, we can stay sober and our subconscious minds do not often bother us. *Am I still conditioning my conscious mind?*

Meditation for the Day

When feeling sympathy and compassion for those in temptation, a condition I sometimes experience, I have a responsibility toward them. Sympathy always includes responsibility. When I am moved with compassion, I should go to the one in need and bind up his or her wounds as best I can.

Prayer for the Day

I pray that I may have compassion for others' trials.

AA Thought for the Day

 An idle thought connected with drinking casually pops into our minds. That is the crucial moment. Will we harbor that thought even for one minute, or will we banish it from our minds at once? If we let it stay, it may develop into a daydream. If we allow the daydream to stay in our minds, it may lead to a decision, however unconscious, to take a drink. *Do I let myself daydream?*

Meditation for the Day

Many of us have a vision of the kind of person God wants us to be. I must be true to my vision, whatever it is, and I must try to live up to it by living the way I believe I should live. There is a good person whom God sees in me, the person I could be and that God would like me to be.

Prayer for the Day

I pray that I may try to fulfill God's vision of what I could be.

AA Thought for the Day

 There is some alcoholic thought, conscious or unconscious, that comes before every slip. As long as we live, we must be on the lookout for such thoughts and guard against them. In fact, our AA training is mostly to prepare us, to make us ready to recognize such thoughts at once and to reject them at once. *How well is my mind prepared?*

Meditation for the Day

Don't trouble my mind with puzzles that I cannot solve. The solutions may never be shown to me until I have left this life. "I have yet many things to say to you, but you cannot bear them now." Only step by step, stage by stage, can I proceed in my journey into greater knowledge and understanding.

Prayer for the Day

I pray that I may be content that things
I now see darkly will some day be made clear.

AA Thought for the Day

 If we allow an alcoholic thought to lodge in our minds for any length of time, we are in danger of having a slip. Therefore we must dispel such thoughts at once, by refusing to let them in and by immediately putting constructive thoughts in their place. Remember that alcohol is poison to us. We need to think of every reason we have learned in AA for not taking that drink. *Am I keeping my thoughts constructive?*

Meditation for the Day

I do not try to get praise and attention from the world. I should be one of those who, though sometimes scoffed at, has a serenity and peace of mind that the scoffers never know.

Prayer for the Day

I pray that I will not pay too much attention to the judgment of the world.

AA Thought for the Day

In spite of all we have learned in AA, our old way of thinking comes back on us, sometimes with overwhelming force, and occasionally some of us have slips. We eventually get drunk. Those who have had slips say unanimously that they were no fun. They say AA had taken all the pleasure out of drinking. *Am I convinced that I can never get anything more out of drinking?*

Meditation for the Day

I give something to those who are having trouble, to those whose thoughts are confused. I give something of my sympathy, my prayers, my time, my love, my thought, my self. Then I give of my own confidence, as I have had it given to me by the grace of God. The giving of advice can never take the place of the giving of myself.

Prayer for the Day

I pray that as I have received, so may I give.

AA Thought for the Day

 People who have had a slip are ashamed of themselves—sometimes so ashamed that they fear going back to AA. They develop the old inferiority complex and tell themselves that they are no good, that they have let down their friends in AA, that they are hopeless, and that they can never make it. But their AA training cannot ever be entirely lost. They know there is still God's help for them if they will again ask for it. *Do I believe that I can never entirely lose what I have learned in AA?*

Meditation for the Day

The first step toward conquering temptation is to see it clearly as temptation. I dissociate myself from it, put it out of my mind as soon as it appears. I do not think of excuses for yielding to it. I turn at once to my Higher Power for help.

Prayer for the Day

I pray that I may be prepared for whatever temptation may come to me.

AA Thought for the Day

 When people come back to AA after having a slip, the temptation is strong to say nothing about it. No other AA should force them to declare themselves. It is entirely up to them. If they are well grounded in AA, they will realize that it's up to them to speak up at the next meeting and tell about their slip. *Am I tolerant of other people's mistakes?*

Meditation for the Day

It is in the union of a soul with God that strength, new life, and spiritual power come. Bread sustains the body, but I cannot live by bread alone. To try to do the will of God is the meat and support of true living. Soul starvation comes from failing to do so. The world talks about bodies that are undernourished. What about the souls that are undernourished?

Prayer for the Day

I pray that my spirit may live by trying to do the will of God as I understand it.

AA Thought for the Day

 The length of time of our sobriety is not as important as its quality. A person who has been in AA for a number of years may not be in as good mental condition as a person who has only been in AA a few months. And the older members must realize that as long as they live, they are only one drink away from a drunk. *What is the quality of my sobriety?*

Meditation for the Day

I can have all the power I need from the unseen God. I can have his grace, his spirit, to make me effective as I go along each day. Opportunities for a better world are all around me. But I do not work alone. The power of God is behind all good works.

Prayer for the Day

I pray that my work may be made more effective by the grace of God.

AA Thought for the Day

Human beings were not meant to live alone. We all need to be by ourselves at times, but we cannot really live without the companionship of others. Our natures demand it. Our lives depend largely upon it. The fellowship of AA seems to us to be the best in the world. *Do I fully appreciate what the fellowship of AA means to me?*

Meditation for the Day

Many of us are at least subconsciously seeking for a Power greater than ourselves because that would give a meaning to our existence. If I have found that Higher Power, I can be the means of leading others, by showing them that their search for a meaning to life will end when they find faith and trust in God as the answer.

Prayer for the Day

I pray that I may find peace of mind in the thought of God and his purpose for my life.

AA Thought for the Day

 Our drinking fellowship was a substitute one, for lack of something better. At the time, we did not realize what real fellowship could be. Drinking fellowship has a fatal fault. It is not based on a firm foundation. Most of it is on the surface. It is based mostly on the desire to use your companions for your own pleasure, and using others is a false foundation. *Do I see my drinking fellowship in its proper light?*

Meditation for the Day

I set for myself the task of growing daily more and more into the consciousness of a Higher Power. This is done by prayer, quiet times, and communion. Often all I need to do is sit silent before God and let him speak to me through my thought. When the guidance comes, I must not hesitate, but go out and follow that guidance in my daily work.

Prayer for the Day

I pray that I may be still
and know that God is with me.

AA Thought for the Day

 Group therapy is directed toward the help that the individual receives from it. It is essentially selfish. It is using the companionship of other alcoholics only in order to stay sober ourselves. But this is only the beginning of real AA fellowship. *Do I deeply feel the true AA fellowship?*

Meditation for the Day

Most of us have had to live through the dark part of our lives, when we were full of struggle and care, worry and remorse, when we felt deeply the tragedy of life. But with a daily surrender to a Higher Power come peace and joy that make all things new. I can now take each day as a joyous sunrise-gift from God to use for him and for other people. The night of the past is gone; this day is mine.

Prayer for the Day

I pray that I may thank God for this day and be glad in it.

AA Thought for the Day

 The clergy speak of the spiritual fellowship of the church. Such a fellowship is based on a common belief in God and a common effort to live a spiritual life. We try to have this in AA. We also try to get down to the real problems in each others' lives. We try to open up to each other. We have a real desire to be of service to each other. *Do I appreciate the deep personal fellowship of AA?*

Meditation for the Day

Love and fear cannot dwell together. Fear is a very strong force. And therefore a weak and wavering love can soon be driven out by fear. But a strong love, a love that trusts in God, is sure eventually to conquer fear. The only sure way to dispel fear is to have the love of God more and more in my heart and soul.

Prayer for the Day

I pray that my fear will flee before the power of the love of God.

AA Thought for the Day

 AA fellowship is partly group therapy. It is partly spiritual fellowship. But it is even more. It goes deep down into our personal lives and needs. It requires a full opening up to each other of our innermost thoughts and most secret problems. In AA we can be sure of sympathy, understanding, and real help. These things make the AA fellowship the best that we know. *Do I fully appreciate the depth of AA fellowship?*

Meditation for the Day

My Higher Power can guide me to the right decisions if I pray about them. I can believe that many details of my life are planned by God and planned with a wealth of forgiving love for the mistakes I have made. I can pray today to be shown the right way. I can choose the good, and when I choose it, I can feel that the whole power of the universe is behind me

Prayer for the Day

I pray that I may be shown the right way to live today.

AA Thought for the Day

 The way of AA is the way of service. Without that, it would not work. Not until we begin to help other people do we get full relief. It is an axiom that the AA program has to be given away in order to be kept. We get and then we give. If we do not give, we do not keep. *Have I given up all ideas of holding AA for myself alone?*

Meditation for the Day

I try to see the life of the spirit as a calm place, shut away from the turmoil of the world. I think of my spiritual home as a place full of peace, serenity, and contentment. I go to this quiet, meditative place for the strength to carry me through today's duties and problems. I keep coming back for refreshment when I am weary of the outside world.

Prayer for the Day

*I pray that I may keep this resting place
where I can commune with God.*

AA Thought for the Day

Service to others makes the world a good place. What a wonderful world it would be if we took our own greatest problem and found the answer to it and spent the rest of our lives helping others with the same problem in our spare time. Soon we would have the right kind of world. *Do I appreciate my unique opportunity to be of service?*

Meditation for the Day

Today I can live in the consciousness of God's contact, which upholds me in all good thoughts, words, and deeds. If sometimes there seems to be a shadow on my life and I feel out of sorts, I remember that this is not the withdrawal of God's presence but only my temporary unwillingness to realize it.

Prayer for the Day

I pray that I may face the dull days with courage.

AA Thought for the Day

The way of AA is the way of faith. We don't get the full benefit of the program until we surrender our lives to some Power greater than ourselves and trust that Power to give us the strength we need. There is no better way for us. We can get sober without it. We can stay sober for some time without it. But if we are going to truly live, we must take the way of faith in God. That is the path for us. We must follow it. *Have I taken the way of faith?*

Meditation for the Day

Life is not a search for happiness. Happiness is a by-product of living the right kind of life, of doing the right thing. If I search for right living, happiness will be my reward.

Prayer for the Day

*I pray that I will not seek happiness
but seek to do right.*

AA Thought for the Day

 The way of faith is, of course, not confined to AA. It is for everybody who really wants to live. But many people can go through life without much of it. Many are doing so, to their own sorrow. Life has no goal for many. They are strangers in the land. They are not at home. But for us in AA, the way of faith is the way of life. We have proved by our past lives that we could not live without it. *Do I think I could live happily without faith?*

Meditation for the Day

"He makes his sun rise on the evil and on the good, and sends rain on the just and on the unjust." God does not interfere with the working of natural laws. The laws of nature are unchangeable, otherwise I could not depend on them. Spiritual laws are also made to be obeyed.

Prayer for the Day

I pray that I may live today with faith and hope and love.

AA Thought for the Day

 Unless we have the key of faith to un-lock the meaning of life, we are lost. We do not choose faith because it is one way for us, but because it is the only way. We cannot live victoriously without faith; we are at sea without a rudder or an anchor, drifting on the sea of life. Our souls are restless until they find rest in God. Without faith, our lives are a meaningless succession of unrelated happenings, without rhyme or rea-son. *Have I come to rest in faith?*

Meditation for the Day

This vast universe around me, including this wonderful earth on which I live, was once per-haps only a thought in the mind of God. I must try to get guidance from the Divine Mind as to what his intention is for the world and what part I can have in carrying out that intention.

Prayer for the Day

I pray that I will not worry over the limitations of my human mind. I pray that I may live as though my mind were a reflection of the Divine Mind.

AA Thought for the Day

 The skeptic says it is impossible for us to find the answer to life. But many more have put aside intellectual pride and have said to themselves, *Who am I to say there is no God? Who am I to say there is no purpose in life?* Others live for the moment and do not think about why they are here or where they are going. *Do I care where I am going?*

Meditation for the Day

I do not need to fear material things, which are neither good nor bad in the moral sense. There seems to be no active force for evil—outside of human beings themselves. Humans alone can have either evil intentions—resentments, malevolence, hate, and revenge—or good intentions—love and goodwill. They can make something ugly or something beautiful out of the clay of their lives.

Prayer for the Day

I pray that I may be a good artisan.

AA Thought for the Day

 When we were drinking, our lives were made up of a lot of scattered and unrelated pieces. We must pick up our lives and put them together again. We do it by recovering faith in a Divine Principle in the universe that holds us together and holds the whole universe together and gives it meaning and purpose. We surrender our disorganized lives to that Power, we get into harmony with the Divine Spirit, and our lives are made whole again. *Is my life whole again?*

Meditation for the Day

I avoid fear as I would a plague. Fear, even the smallest fear, is a hacking at the cords of faith that bind me to God. However small the fraying, in time those cords will wear thin, and then one disappointment or shock will make them snap. All fear is disloyalty to God. It is a denial of his care and protection.

Prayer for the Day

I pray that I may have such trust in God today that I will not fear anything too much.

AA Thought for the Day

Have we ceased being inwardly defeated, at war with ourselves? Have we given ourselves freely to AA and to the Higher Power? Have we gotten over being sick inside? We have learned how the program works. Now will we follow it with all we have, with all we can give, with all our might, with all our life? *Am I going to let AA principles guide the rest of my life?*

Meditation for the Day

In all decisions to be made today, I yield to the gentle pressure of my conscience. I take the events of today as part of God's planning and ordering. I wait quietly until I have an inner urge, a leading, a feeling that a thing is right, a pressure on my will by the spirit of God.

Prayer for the Day

I pray that today I may try to follow the inner pressure of God's leading.

AA Thought for the Day

As we look back over our drinking careers, we must realize that our lives were a mess because we were a mess inside. The trouble was in us, not in life itself. Life itself was good enough, but we were looking at it the wrong way. We were in a house with one-way glass in the windows. People could see us, but we could not look out and see them and see what life meant to them and should mean to us. *Can I now look at life as it really is?*

Meditation for the Day

I will fear no evil, because the power of God can conquer evil. Evil has power to seriously hurt only those who do not place themselves under the protection of the Higher Power. This is not a question of feeling, it is an assured fact of my experience. I can be sure of the protection of God's grace.

Prayer for the Day

I pray that I may try to place myself today under the protection of God's grace.

AA Thought for the Day

We have definitely left that dream world behind. It was only a sham. It was a world of our making, and it was not the real world. We are sorry for the past, yes, but we learned a lot from it. It has given us the knowledge necessary to face the world as it really is. We had to become alcoholics in order to find the AA program. We would not have gotten it any other way. *Do I look at my past as valuable experience?*

Meditation for the Day

I need to spread peace, not discord, wherever I go. I try to be part of the cure of every situation, not part of the problem. I try to ignore evil, rather than to actively combat it. I always try to build up, never to tear down.

Prayer for the Day

I pray that I may try to bring something good into every situation today.

AA Thought for the Day

 Many people live good lives from their youth on, not getting into serious trouble, being well adjusted to life, and yet they have not found all that we drunks have found. We had the good fortune to find Alcoholics Anonymous and with it a new life. We are among the lucky few in the world who have learned a new way to live. *Am I deeply grateful for the new life that I have learned in AA?*

Meditation for the Day

A deep gratitude to my Higher Power for all the blessings that I have and that I don't deserve has come to me. I thank God and mean it. Then comes service to other people, out of gratitude for what I have received. This entails some sacrifice of myself and my own affairs. But I am glad to do it. Gratitude, service, and then sacrifice are the steps that lead to good AA work. They open the door to a new life.

Prayer for the Day

I pray that I may keep a deep sense of obligation.

AA Thought for the Day

 Many alcoholics will be saying today, "This is a good Christmas for me." They will be looking back over past Christmases that were not like this one. They will be thanking God for their sobriety and their newfound life. *Is this a happy Christmas for me?*

Meditation for the Day

"They offered him gifts—gold, frankincense, and myrrh." I bring my gifts of gold—my money and material possessions. I bring my frankincense—the consecration of my life to a worthy cause. I bring my myrrh—my sympathy and understanding and help. I lay them all at the feet of God and let him have full use of them.

Prayer for the Day

I pray that I may bring my gifts
and lay them on the altar.

AA Thought for the Day

We are glad to be a part of AA. We are glad to be able to be useful, to have a reason for living, a purpose in life. We want to lose our lives in this great cause and so find it again. *Am I grateful to be an AA?*

Meditation for the Day

These meditations can teach me how to relax. I can go along through life doing the best I can, but without a feeling of urgency or strain. I can enjoy all the good things and the beauty of life, but at the same time depend deeply on God.

Prayer for the Day

I pray that I may enjoy the satisfaction that comes from good work well done.

AA Thought for the Day

We need AA for the development of the buried life within us. This life within us is developing slowly but surely, with many setbacks, mistakes, failures. As long as we stick close to AA, this life will go on developing. We cannot yet know what it will be, but we know that it will be good. That's all we want to know. *Am I thanking God for AA?*

Meditation for the Day

I build my life on the firm foundation of true gratitude to God for all his blessings and true humility because of my unworthiness of these blessings.

Prayer for the Day

I pray that I may build my life on AA principles.

AA Thought for the Day

 AA may be human in its organization, but it is divine in its purpose. The purpose is to point us toward God and the good life. Our feet have been set upon the right path. We feel it in the depths of our being. We are going in the right direction. The future can be safely left to God. *Am I pointed toward God and the good life?*

Meditation for the Day

Although unseen, God is always near to those who believe in him and trust him and depend on him for the strength to meet the challenges of life. The feeling that God is with me should not depend on any passing mood of mine; I should try to be always conscious of his power and love in the background of my life.

Prayer for the Day

I pray that I may feel that God is not too far away to depend on for help.

AA Thought for the Day

 Participating in the privileges of the movement, we shall share in the responsibilities, taking it upon ourselves to carry our fair share of the load, not grudgingly but joyfully. We are deeply grateful for the privileges we enjoy because of our membership in this great movement. *Will I accept every opportunity gladly?*

Meditation for the Day

Work and prayer are the two forces that are gradually making a better world. I must work for the betterment of myself and other people. "Faith without works is dead." But all work with people should be based on prayer. If I say a little prayer before I speak or try to help, it will make me more effective.

Prayer for the Day

*I pray that I will not work without prayer
or pray without work.*

AA Thought for the Day

To the extent that we fail in our responsibilities, AA fails. To the extent that we succeed, AA succeeds. Every one of our failures will set back AA work to that extent. Every one of our successes will put AA ahead to that extent. *Will I accept every challenge gladly?*

Meditation for the Day

People are failures in the deepest sense when they seek to live without God's sustaining power. Many people try to be self-sufficient and seek selfish pleasure and find that it does not work too well. No matter how much material wealth they acquire, no matter how much fame, the time of disillusionment and futility usually comes. What does it matter if I have gained the whole world, but lost my own soul?

Prayer for the Day

I pray that I may so live that I will not be afraid to die.

AA Thought for the Day

We shall be loyal in our attendance, generous in our giving, kind in our criticism, creative in our suggestions, loving in our attitudes. We shall give AA our interest, our enthusiasm, our devotion, and most of all, ourselves. *Have I given myself?*

Meditation for the Day

As I look back over the year just gone, I can feel satisfied that it has been a good year to the extent that I have put good thoughts, good words, and good deeds into it. None of what I have thought, said, or done need be wasted. I can profit from both the good and the bad experiences. I can humbly thank God for the good things of the year that has passed.

Prayer for the Day

I pray that I may carry on with faith,
with prayer, and with hope.

The Serenity Prayer

God grant me the serenity
To accept the things I cannot change,
The courage to change the things I can,
And the wisdom to know the difference.

The Twelve Steps of
Alcoholics Anonymous*

1. We admitted we were powerless over alcohol—that our lives had become unmanageable.
2. Came to believe that a Power greater than ourselves could restore us to sanity.
3. Made a decision to turn our will and our lives over to the care of God *as we understood Him.*
4. Made a searching and fearless moral inventory of ourselves.
5. Admitted to God, to ourselves, and to another human being the exact nature of our wrongs.
6. Were entirely ready to have God remove all these defects of character.
7. Humbly asked Him to remove our shortcomings.
8. Made a list of all persons we had harmed, and became willing to make amends to them all.
9. Made direct amends to such people wherever possible, except when to do so would injure them or others.
10. Continued to take personal inventory and when we were wrong promptly admitted it.
11. Sought through prayer and meditation to improve our conscious contact with God *as we understood Him*, praying only for knowledge of His will for us and the power to carry that out.
12. Having had a spiritual awakening as the result of these steps, we tried to carry this message to alcoholics, and to practice these principles in all our affairs.

*The Twelve Steps of AA are taken from *Alcoholics Anonymous*, 3d ed., published by AA World Services, Inc., New York, N.Y., 59–60.

The Twelve Traditions of Alcoholics Anonymous*

1. Our common welfare should come first; personal recovery depends upon A.A. unity.

2. For our group purpose there is but one ultimate authority—a loving God as He may express Himself in our group conscience. Our leaders are but trusted servants; they do not govern.

3. The only requirement for A.A. membership is a desire to stop drinking.

4. Each group should be autonomous except in matters affecting other groups or A.A. as a whole.

5. Each group has but one primary purpose—to carry its message to the alcoholic who still suffers.

6. An A.A. group ought never endorse, finance or lend the A.A. name to any related facility or outside enterprise, lest problems of money, property and prestige divert us from our primary purpose.

7. Every A.A. group ought to be fully self-supporting, declining outside contributions.

8. Alcoholics Anonymous should remain forever nonprofessional, but our service centers may employ special workers.

9. A.A., as such, ought never to be organized; but we may create service boards or committees directly responsible to those they serve.

10. Alcoholics Anonymous has no opinion on outside issues; hence the A.A. name ought never be drawn into public controversy.

11. Our public relations policy is based on attraction rather than promotion; we need always maintain personal anonymity at the level of press, radio and films.

12. Anonymity is the spiritual foundation of all our Traditions, ever reminding us to place principles before personalities.

*The Twelve Traditions of AA are taken from *Alcoholics Anonymous*, 3d ed., published by AA World Services, Inc., New York, N.Y., 564.

Index

A

C

D

E

H

I

M

N

O

P

Q

L. Loyalty to all or one group? Listening well? Faithful to AA movement? Letters I should write? Laziness? Listening to the long-winded speaker?

M. Meeting attendance regular?

N. Newcomers welcomed? Neglecting responsibilities?

O. Opening up to the isolated? Obligations in order?

P. Pride in fellowship? Procrastination over with? Purposes in life?

Q. Questioning newcomers' seriousness?

R. Responsibilities up to par in program? Repaying debts?

S. Self-consciousness holding you back? A+ sharing? Superiority? Sponsoring skills okay? Serious commitment? Too sensitive? Self-satisfying?

T. Tolerance? Will there really be a tomorrow? Time left? Taking action?

U. Usefulness to the program? Ugly thoughts about other people?

V. Continual volunteering? Yourself as victim? Self-victim?

W. Work sharing? Wasted past life?

X. Xenophobia subsiding?

Y. Yearnings for others' possessions? For others? Yelling in control? "Yes-man" syndrome leaving? Tolerance of youthful interpretations?

Z. Zero tolerance improving? Zigzag brain improving? Zest for life returning? Zooming ninety miles an hour?

R

S

Y

T